FREE
MEDICINE

ALSO BY PIR ELIAS AMIDON

Earth Prayers: 365 Prayers, Poems,
and Invocations from Around the World
(Elizabeth Roberts, co-editor)

Honoring the Earth: A Journal of New Earth Prayers
(Elizabeth Roberts, co-editor)

Life Prayers: 365 Prayers, Blessings, and
Affirmations to Celebrate the Human Journey
(Elizabeth Roberts, co-editor)

Prayers for a Thousand Years
(Elizabeth Roberts, co-editor)

The Open Path: Recognizing Nondual Awareness

FREE
MEDICINE

MEDITATIONS ON NONDUAL AWAKENING

PIR ELIAS AMIDON

SENTIENT PUBLICATIONS

First Sentient Publications edition 2016
Copyright © 2016 by Elias Amidon

For permissions, see page 139.

A paperback original

Cover design by Kim Johansen, Black Dog Design, www.blackdogdesign.com
Book design by Black Dog Design

Library of Congress Cataloging-in-Publication Data

Names: Amidon, Elias, author.
Title: Free medicine : meditations on nondual awakening / Pir Elias Amidon.
Description: 1st ed. | Boulder, Colorado : Sentient Publications, LLC, 2016.
Identifiers: LCCN 2016017685 | ISBN 9781591812852
Subjects: LCSH: Awareness--Religious aspects. | Spiritual life. |
    Meditations. | Sufism.
Classification: LCC BL629.5.A82 A44 2016 | DDC 204/.4--dc23 LC record
available at https://lccn.loc.gov/2016017685

Printed in the United States of America

10 9 8 7 6 5 4 3 2 1

SENTIENTPUBLICATIONS
A Limited Liability Company
PO Box 7204
Boulder, CO 80306
www.sentientpublications.com

for you

CONTENTS

—•••—

A Note to Those Who Open This Book

THIS BOOK IS A COMPANION FOR THOSE whose deepest desire is to experience first-hand the good news at the heart of reality. This good news is not hidden — it's revealed in the ceaseless spontaneity of the present moment — but opening to a direct experience of it requires a process of "self-erasure" that can be difficult to allow. Relaxing into the transparency of one's self can bring fear, and we can easily pull back behind familiar borders without knowing it, or get caught up in spiritual ambition and lose the freshness of presence that's at the heart of this. Hence the need for companions like this book, or like many other books in this vein, or better yet, for a human companion who can remind us of what we have forgotten.

I recommend reading *Free Medicine* in small doses — perhaps keep the book on your bedside table, read one or two pieces a night, or just open it at random and read what you find, and then close the book again.

These short pieces have been written over the past five years for students and others interested in what I call the Open Path, a path of nondual awakening. Inasmuch as the Open Path offers guidance, it does take the form of a spiritual path; however, since that form is fundamentally open, the path vanishes as we travel it. The Open Path belongs to all of us. It is not defined by religious beliefs or owned by any tradition. It belongs to all of us because it is present *right now,* for everyone, in the indefinable freshness of the moment.

Many diverse themes are explored here. What unifies them all is their allegiance to "the good news at the heart of reality," and to directly experiencing that good news rather than simply philosophizing about it. The good news itself is unspeakable. Words can only orbit around it, doing what they can to point to it, but ultimately they must await the serendipitous arrival of grace — and when that might happen is anyone's guess. The most we can do, in the words of the Sufi master Ibn 'Arabi, is "put ourselves in the way of it." That's the intention of this book: to put the reader in the way of grace.

My own spiritual path has been influenced by many traditions. Although I was initiated in a Sufi order nearly fifty years ago and continue to teach in that tradition, the style of Sufism I try to express is ecumenical rather than sectarian. My conviction is that we humans share an ancient and universal mystical impulse. We've inherited it from countless generations of ancestors who, like us, looked out on this world, and into the mystery of their own presence, and wondered where all this came from, wondered if there is a truth hidden within the world we perceive that might reveal our true identity, and how it is that we belong here.

We live in an extraordinary and dangerous time. In the past century and a half, humanity has expanded its numbers from less than one billion to over seven billion. We keep multiplying and demanding more sustenance and material comforts from our generous and fragile planet. We even talk now of migrating to other planets, since it's obvious we're hell-bent on trashing this one. But even if we could fly off to other planets verdant enough to support us, we wouldn't deserve them. Without knowing who we are and how it is we belong here, we will never grace any planet with our presence.

We do belong here. We belong together. We belong with the great community of life on earth. We belong in the cosmos, and in the heart of All Being. Our belonging is immanent and self-evident in this moment. Experiencing the immediacy of this revelation is the deepest desire of these writings.

Homage to the One

To this transparent light, clearness itself, omnipresent as space,
to This, the host of all that appears,
to This, the non-locatable, spontaneous here-and-now,
to This that is identical with the openness of all those who,
whether known or unknown, have recognized its simple presence;
to This, our vibrant home, never created
so never able to cease,
to this unseen light, the most familiar presence of now,
indistinguishable from the bones in our face
and the tongue in our mouth,
indistinguishable from our most intimate thoughts and feelings,
yet beyond all limitation,
to this infinite kindness that allows everything to appear,
we bow down.

Caught here, believing we are something,
believing we are something that could be alone,
believing we are these frail, beautiful bodies,
we look for love from each other,
all the while we are made of love.

To which direction shall we bow,
to what sacred place, shrine or God,
if not to the bowing itself?

Bow down, we bow down,
the thunder perfect mind is our own!

What candle shall we light, on what altar,
to this that lights the candle,
and is the candle, and the light?

The Desire to Be at the End of Distances

I REMEMBER MYSELF AS A CHILD waking up in the treetops. My bed was snugged up against a window, so when I opened my eyes in the morning my entire view was of the tall crowns of beech trees, their leaves golden-green and fluttering in the early morning light. Looking at them made me feel safe. I felt as if I didn't have to go anywhere else. There was a friendliness there: me and the treetops. I was home.

Invariably, though, my reverie would come to an end and I would get up. I sometimes wondered why I got up, since nothing that followed in my day ever gave me a truer sense of home than being with the trees in my bed did. There were always distances to travel: distances to go downstairs, distances to finish my breakfast, distances to walk to school, distances to wait for summer vacation to start, distances to go until I grew up. In my bed in the treetops there were no distances.

As I got bigger I would climb those trees and sit alone in their smooth branches. Being alone up there was home. But always I would have to climb down and join the distances again.

Gradually my life became a traveling of distances. I rode my bicycle to the sea, a long distance, and when I arrived I looked out on its grey frothy surface and saw only distances. I learned to kiss my girlfriend, and the winning of that kiss revealed the breathless distances our bodies had yet to travel. I rode my little motor scooter across America to San Francisco, and finally arriving there, I saw the distances to Japan and New York.

I felt the small, daily distances layering into larger ones, and those forming part of ever-larger ones. There was no end to them: each moment was a distance to the next, the cracking of an egg a distance to its eating, the planning of a project a distance to its completion. Things never really arrived; they just led to more distances.

So I traveled to a spiritual teacher, thinking that crossing that distance would finally bring me home – but again, I only saw more distances. Years of practice and meditation followed, things to understand, spiritual levels to attain, the distance to enlightenment enormous in my imagination.

That's not to say I was never "in the moment." I was. My moments were made of the delicious, confusing signals of a sensate body and a curious mind. But where was the payoff? Where was the place where everything was resolved? Where was the end of distances? Where was home?

The young boy at home in the fluttering golden-green leaves, the young boy with nowhere else to go, is now a white-haired man. My desire for the end of distances has gradually vanished. It has vanished through the intercession of hundreds of little graces inviting me to simply accept what is, as it is. No struggle.

Though it seeks intimacy, the desire to be at the end of distances is the very thing that maintains them, and their loneliness. Wanting something that is not yet here; not wanting something that is here; wanting things to change; not wanting things to change – these wantings create the span of distances themselves.

Home is not what I had imagined. It is not a place of arrival. Seeking to arrive at the end of distances, whether to a place of security, or success, or embrace of love, or spiritual epiphany, is to remain unfulfilled. The end of distances is the end of seeking them.

Of course, distances still appear to me, but now they end where they begin, in this intimacy. For example, as I write this there is the distance between these words and what I am trying to say — but this is the distance of love-play, not waiting.

Another way to say it might be that distances open in every direction, but now they simply move through me; I am not going anywhere. I neither dwell in a "here" at the beginning of a distance nor seek a place of safety or resolution that I imagine at the end of one. There is no "here" or "there." There is just home where I am, a home with no walls, which makes it as much yours as mine.

("The desire to be at the end of distances" is a line from Wallace Stevens' poem "The Rock.")

The Everyday Practice

AS A YOUNG MAN SEARCHING FOR TRUTH I found a Sufi order and asked for instruction. My teacher gave me a series of practices, among which was a simple breathing prayer: "Open me Lord, and let me flow." I was told to silently repeat on my in-breath, "Open me Lord," and on my out-breath, "and let me flow."

I took this practice to heart, repeating it whenever I remembered — sitting on my cushion, walking down a street, opening a door, preparing a meal, raising a spoonful of soup to my mouth. *Open me Lord, and let me flow.*

Unlike many in my generation, I didn't have a problem with the word "Lord." I wasn't raised in a theistic tradition, so the word didn't resonate for me with authoritarian patriarchy — it just signified everything I didn't understand about reality, all the awesome forces at work in the universe. Since I was a typical young man tangled up in my thoughts and emotions, I had no confidence that I could open myself, but "Lord" — this incomprehensible power behind all things — to this I could appeal and submit. *Open me Lord. Let me flow.*

I repeated the prayer so often that the words became transparent to me, leaving just a visceral motion of opening whenever I breathed with this intention — like a swing swinging in the open air. It became "my familiar," and still is.

Visiting a friend's house recently, I saw these words from Chögyam Trungpa Rinpoche written in a framed calligraphy:

The everyday practice is simply to develop a complete acceptance and openness to all situations and emotions, and to all people, experiencing everything totally without mental reservations and blockages, so that one never withdraws or centralizes into oneself.

There it was. The teaching of my little breathing prayer was inscribed in Trungpa's sentence. His words don't tell you how to respond to all situations and emotions, they don't give you any moral guidance. They simply indicate the naked openness by which life can be lived most authentically.

The final phrase is particularly penetrating: "...so that one never withdraws or centralizes into oneself." How familiar is this movement of withdrawing and centralizing into oneself! Don't we do it a thousand times each day? Things get hectic, we're late to work, someone cuts us off, someone criticizes us, our family takes us for granted, we feel inadequate, or lonely, or without a meaningful future. Centralized into our self, we join the world's neurotic drama. But at least we think we know what's happening; we have a point of view.

It takes profound trust to open from our solid point of view, from our withdrawal. Perhaps this is the utility of the word "Lord" — surrendering to universal forces you don't understand, that are beyond your point of view. *Open me Lord.*

But there is something strange here. Who is the "me" that is opened and that flows? When the *me* opens, is it any longer a *me?* When the *me* flows, what flows?

Here is the heart of this everyday practice. This is where it changes from words and good advice to in-your-face truth. Here we have to stop thinking, and look for ourselves. What "me" opens?

When we look, we don't find anything! There is simply clear, open awareness, immediate and naturally occurring.

Shabkar Lama, a nineteenth-century mystic-minstrel of the Tibetan plateau, speaks to this same question: What "me" opens?

> *Do not look at the vision but look for the viewer. Looking for the viewer, if you fail to find him, then your vision is at the point of resolution. This vision in which there is nothing at all to see but which is not a blank nothingness, is vivid and unalloyed perception of the here and now...*

No viewer, no meditator, no actor, no me, and finally, no Lord! Just this vivid openness, free of a *me,* free of withdrawal into a *myself.* This freedom is what flows, all by itself. Breathing, now: *Open me Lord, and let me flow.*

The First Moment

THE CLOCK TICKS. THE SUN RISES. Today takes the place of yesterday. This breath gives itself up to this one. My pen point moves across the paper, your eye moves across the words, each moment giving up, letting go.

Letting go is the gift of emptiness, and the genesis of you and me at this moment. How intimate it is! Always beginning by letting go. "The place of release is where it all begins," a Tibetan scripture, *The Garland of Pearls,* tells us. We appear this moment by the grace of the previous moment's vanishing. This is not done once, but always. It is the most common miracle — the entire cosmos refreshing itself every instant.

"Nirvana," Nagarjuna wrote, "is the letting go of what arises and passes." This means nirvana — what we might translate as "refreshing ease" — is present in the way each moment so easily offers itself up, refreshing everything by letting go. In Zen and Dzogchen teachings, the mystery of this simultaneous vanishing and appearing is called "the first moment."

The first moment is prior to our thoughts about it. Our ideas can't touch it. It is the empty clearing that is so close we can't see it. We can't see it, we can't think it, and yet the first moment is the most intimate and immediate mystery we share with the whole universe.

Even though we can't see the first moment, our life practice must be to never lose sight of it. That is, the letting go that is emptiness must become familiar and present in the same way that space or gravity is familiar and present. We must let letting go wash us of our fixed ideas. Luckily the whole universe is working this way, so we have help.

But our life practice isn't only about opening ourselves to the flow of letting go. Simultaneously we are created. There is no gap between emptiness — letting go — and our appearing as we do. The universe spontaneously appears in its wholeness, including you and me, in this instant. This spontaneity is one way to sense our interdependence with all events everywhere. Everything appears simultaneously now, born of the first moment.

To the extent we experience ourselves to be the intersection of emptiness and appearance, our life practice is working. While it takes utter resolve on our part to recognize this, the practice itself is effortless since it's how everything is happening already. Our resolve is not a strain, or something we make happen. It is pure faith, radiant in every atom of our being. All we have to do is let go and open.

Opening in the first moment, we can be completely devoted to our life; we can take care of it tenderly and wisely. Opening and gliding in the first moment, there is no sense of being a separate existence, a self trying to have its way in the midst of everything else. Our responsiveness to what occurs is sensitive and easy-going. Here we are not at fault, nor can we take credit for what we do. Here we are calm, though everything is changing and letting go.

Our body moves gracefully. Our thoughts and gestures are generous. In the first moment we have nothing to lose. Our happiness is without cause.

Surrender That Thought

WHAT IS IT THAT MAKES US FEEL uneasy, worried, angry, defensive, jealous, or judgmental? Is it really because conditions in the world around us, and the actions of people we encounter, make us feel these feelings? Or is there something else at work?

When we look into the nature of what Buddhists call "afflictive emotions" like these, the first thing we notice is that they are accompanied by thoughts. For example, consider this thought-stream: *My boyfriend is not as attentive as he used to be. I saw him looking at that other girl. He's probably going to leave me. It will be terrible. No one will ever want to be with me. I'll be alone forever.* Thoughts like these pile up and we start believing them. This is one way the fearful ego convinces itself it is something substantial: by reiterating points of view about the fickle, dangerous conditions of the world. The self-as-victim now has a place to live. As long as it clings to its beliefs and fears, its "position" is assured.

Notice that it's not the thoughts themselves, but our *sticking* to them that generates the afflictive emotions. If we don't grasp onto these kinds of thoughts, they lose their charge; they no longer have the power to fuel our emotional and psychological suffering.

You can check this out for yourself by recalling a time in the past when you felt anxious or jealous or angry about something. Notice that now you don't feel those feelings. Why? Because you are no longer in the grip of the thoughts that accompanied them; they simply don't matter to you anymore. Over time, they have lost their charge.

This simple dynamic — that clinging to our thoughts generates and maintains emotional and psychological suffering — might give us a clue about how to relieve these discomforts. But first we need to look a little deeper into the nature of thoughts themselves, and how it is we stick to them.

We humans think a lot, but do we really know what thinking is? Do we know how we think? Let's try a little experiment here: imagine something, anything, and see if you can find where that thought came from. Did you "create" it? How? Why did that particular thought appear and not a different one? Look carefully. See if you can discover the exact place or moment in which you "make" a specific thought.

As I attempt this myself, looking to see how I discover the next words in this sentence, I can't find how I do it. First the word is not there, and then it is. Sometimes a word arises and it seems okay, but after a few moments I discover it is not exactly right, and I try another word or phrase. The new word or phrase appears just as magically as the first one, out of nowhere!

Here's another seemingly magical quality of thought: watch the stream of thoughts in your mind and see if you can find where a particular thought goes after it's finished. What do you find? It vanishes! The little thought leaves no trace, simply dissolving into thin air.

If you've stayed with this thought experiment so far, you might see that your thoughts are less substantial than you assumed. They come out of nowhere and vanish into nowhere.

This insubstantiality of thoughts is easy to see with the random thoughts of our experiment, but it is much more difficult to see with thoughts that "matter," thoughts we believe in and cling to. When our thoughts tell us we're not good enough, or that we have to improve ourselves, or that other people are not good enough, or this is to blame, or that is wrong, or something bad might happen, these kinds of thoughts "hook" us.

Huang Po, the ninth-century Zen master, once remarked, "Your sole concern should be, as thought succeeds thought, to avoid clinging to any of them."

How can we do that? How can we avoid clinging to our thoughts, especially when our well-being seems to be at stake? Here is where it's helpful to apply a simple practice, first with less important thoughts, and then with the ones we firmly believe in.

I call this practice *"Surrender that thought."* You might wish to try it now, after you finish reading the rest of this paragraph. Simply pause for a few moments, resting in your natural, clear state of mind. Wait. At some point you will notice that a thought is happening. As soon as you notice it, no matter what it is about, surrender your interest in it. I don't mean that you should try to stop the thought from happening or deny it. Just let go of your interest in it. (If you believe it's a really important thought and you feel you can't afford to let go of your interest in it, tell yourself you'll pick it up again in five minutes.) Surrender that thought. Simply let it go; relinquish your interest in it; abandon your belief in its primacy, in its importance and impact on "you." Now notice carefully what happens.

In the instant of surrendering your interest in the thought, you may notice that a subtle sense of openness arises. This sense may be quite brief — another thought may quickly take its place, even the thought: "Oh look! A sense of openness!" So venture again into surrendering that thought, and the next, and the next. This need not require effort — the surrendering we're contemplating here doesn't take any energy or even intention. Just drop your interest in the contents of your thought-stream.

It's a profound experiment, worth exploring on your own in any situation. You might be concerned that by surrendering your thinking mind like this you would become blank, or not understand what's happening, or be unprepared for what is being asked of you. But as you become familiar with this thought-surrendering dynamic you will find a different kind of knowing shows up.

Becoming fluent with this practice, you may discover that in addition to experiencing a sense of openness, spaciousness and silence when you release your interest in the thought, you also experience a kind of relief, even a sense of joy. This joy doesn't have to do with anything — it has no cause. It is the joy intrinsic to clear, open awareness. The need to figure things out is left behind. For a moment, or longer, you find yourself in a space of unknowing which is clear, open presence. As the Dalai Lama said, "I sit at the table of unknowing and invite you to join me here."

Once you become familiar with surrendering less important thoughts, you can explore surrendering ones you have more investment in. For example, say you are at a party and you are participating in a conversation with a group of people. You say something that someone else responds to critically or jokingly. You notice a sinking feeling in your stomach and the stream of thoughts that start proliferating in your mind: *I knew that person doesn't like me; she's so bitchy; now the others will join in the attack on me; I'm such an idiot, why did I say anything? I hate this party;* and so on. As soon as you notice these kinds of thoughts showing up, surrender them. Abandon your interest in them. Unhook from them. Nothing else needs to happen. In the openness of unknowing, you are completely safe and innocent. You have no need to defend yourself or judge anyone. You are the clear presence that you are. Just that.

Instead of conditioning the next moment with troubled thoughts, you surrender your investment in them; now the next moment is open, untroubled, and free. There is no need to judge the world around you; you simply allow it to be what it is. If the situation calls for a response from you, fine; you respond, not from defensiveness or judgment, but from the natural ease of your presence. In the quiet mystery of surrendering your thoughts, you have released any fixity of belief or position-taking, and you are welcomed by openness, quiet, and a most subtle joy — a lightness of being. In surrendering something of no real value, you have gained the world.

The Breath of
the Median Void

Music is what happens between the notes.
— Debussy

I SIT HERE AT DAWN LISTENING TO the city awaken. My neighbor's footsteps on his front stairs. A car door closing. The first traffic on the street, tires on pavement. A bus pulls up outside, the squeak of its brakes as it stops, a little hiss, and the rattle of its engine as it waits. The electric hum of the refrigerator in the kitchen.

Above my head a few dozen miles the air thins to nothing. It is quiet. The silence up there goes on into space forever. Beneath me, beneath this building, in the rock down there, it is quiet. My life is played between two silences, hidden from me.

My body breathes. I don't do anything. This breath is not the breath that preceded it and it is not the one that follows. It is already gone.

I don't know where it has gone, or where it came from. Hidden. I wonder what I am. I look, for the millionth time. Nothing there. I can't find what's thinking this thought. My interiority seems continuous, but there's nothing in there. Whatever it is, it's hidden from me.

I seem to be that which arises at the intersection of something and nothing, the intersection of what is revealed right now and what is hidden right now. My living moment is here — in this space — where the hidden and the revealed encounter each other.

Is it a space? Here where the hidden and the revealed encounter each other, where my breath appears and vanishes, where I am neither something nor nothing, is there any dimension? I look. I don't find any dimension. Yet it seems vast, beyond even the sense of distance.

This is the space Taoists call *the Breath of the Median Void*. It is fundamental, they say, to the Great Breath *(qi)* that animates the living universe. The Breath of the Median Void arises where the Yang Breath — the power of the active (the revealed) — encounters the Yin Breath — the power of the receptive (the hidden). Here. Where I am, without being anything.

Every joy and every sorrow, everything that makes my life worth living occurs here, in the Breath of the Median Void. Everything. When I pick up my little grandson and he lays his head on my shoulder, that gesture meets the silence of the eternal — right there on my shoulder. He and I, nothing in ourselves, touch.

How beautiful this life is — the pleasures, the awakenings, even the losses and the grief. All of it revealed to us, and summed up in this moment now, and swept into the hidden. Utterly vanished. What is left? What remains where the hidden and the revealed meet? What remains is *this* — this living, breathing void… this living, breathing love.

A Garden Among
the Flames

SOMETIMES AS THE DAYS PASS BY — ordinary, uneventful days — we might be visited with the feeling that we're missing something, that there must be more to life than this. We get out of bed in the morning and go through our routine much the same as we did yesterday and much the same as we will tomorrow, and as day follows day we can feel dulled by a kind of weariness, a lack of intimacy, a shallowness of contact with the people and events of our life.

Sufis call this low-level despondency "the fire." It's a fire on low burn to be sure, but add fuel to it — trouble at work, a quarrel with your husband, money problems, a suspicious swelling on your body — and the flames rise. Add even more fuel — you lose your job, your wife leaves you, you receive a terminal diagnosis — and your whole life awakens in fire.

In a famous poem by Ibn 'Arabi, "Gentle Now, Doves," we find these lines:

Pasture between breastbone
and innards.
Marvel!
a garden among the flames!

Breastbone and innards are this embodied life, in flames. There's no way we can totally put out that fire — it's what embodiment does: burn. Even our satisfactions and momentary pleasures burn up, along with everything else that is dear to us.

And yet, wonder of wonders! "A grace like new clothes thrown across the garden!" Rumi shouts, "free medicine for everybody!" A garden among the flames!

What? What grace? What garden?

Ibn 'Arabi points between breastbone and innards to an invisible pasture — *the heart* — that takes up no space (after all, how much space is there between your breastbone and innards?) This "heart pasture," where is it really? In your chest? In the fire? Is it here? Is it over there?

Sufi literature employs the image of the heart, and "the eye of the heart," to signify the seat of the indefinable, primordial, spontaneous presence, the place of what is called "the secret" and "the secret of the secret." Naming it like this aids Sufis in teaching and in writing love poetry, but names only go so far. The names we attribute to notions like "the heart" or "the secret" can't avoid reinforcing the belief that there is, in this case, a quality *over there* called "the heart" that I can perceive from *over here,* thus keeping dominant the dualism of subject-object, self and other.

But in the next line of his poem, Ibn 'Arabi tells the secret:

My heart can take on any form…

My heart can take on any form to the extent that it can relax into its basic openness, its clear spaciousness, the spaciousness that spontaneously appears as everything everywhere. If you look gently into the heart quality of your being, right now, you can sense this spaciousness. In a way of speaking, "my" heart and "your" heart are like windows looking into this infinite heart that holds, and shows up as, the whole cosmos. We live within this heart and can never be exiled from it.

That is how, in the heart's pasture, the seeming division of reality into this over here and that over there, becomes transparent. The flames and the garden are not in opposition. Me and my dreary days, me and my money problems, me and my terminal diagnosis are not in opposition to each other. It's all happening at once and it's not going anywhere — the extraordinary display of light forms arising in the heart's spaciousness.

> *My heart can take on any form:*
> *for gazelles a meadow,*
> *a cloister for monks,*
>
> *For the idols, sacred ground,*
> *Ka'ba for the circling pilgrim,*
> *the tables of the Torah,*
> *the scrolls of the Quran.*

If we look at a stranger walking down the street, or at a squirrel in the tree jumping from branch to branch, or imagine a mother in her clay hut in Sudan, gazing down at her nursing infant's face —

if we let the invisible garden of our heart envelope them, letting this be becomes unconditional, effortless love. It's effortless because it's what's already happening — what we call love is the grace, the force, by which everything appears.

Ibn 'Arabi concludes his poem with this creed:

> *I profess the religion of love.*
> *Wherever its caravan turns*
> *along the way, that is the belief,*
> *the faith I keep.*

The flames of embodiment that hurt — our despondency, anxiety, grief, and loss — don't stop appearing, but we see through them. We see that there is no other. "Yours," "mine," "his," "hers," "here," "there," are transparent designations, momentary flames flickering in the shoreless heart-ocean, right here between breastbone and innards.

Face to Face
with the Bad Guys

SOME YEARS AGO MY WIFE, RABIA, and I had just returned to Rangoon from one of our many journeys to Kachin State in northern Burma. At that time we were conducting a series of trainings for leaders of the indigenous Kachin people in strategies for protecting their lands and waterways. The Kachin had recently emerged from a 35-year civil war with the Burmese military dictatorship — a war the Kachin lost. Business interests from China, Thailand, Indonesia, and the Burmese junta had begun exploiting the natural resources of Kachin lands, one of the richest remaining areas of bio-diversity in the world. Old growth forests were being felled, tigers were being slaughtered, gold mines were leaching arsenic into the rivers, new roads into China were being built, and the Kachin had no say in what was happening.

The sight of armed soldiers was common, both in Kachin State and Rangoon. Whenever I'd see them my heart would recoil —

they were the bad guys I used to see in black-and-white war movies when I was young. To me, they seemed ruthless, inscrutable and frightening. I avoided them whenever possible.

Arriving back in Rangoon after three weeks in the north, we were tired and glad to be back. The morning after our arrival we climbed up the long series of steps to the great Shwedegon Pagoda overlooking Rangoon — the Golden Pagoda — said to have been built during the Buddha's lifetime 2500 years ago.

We went to pay our respects to the place and to give thanks for our safe return. We wandered around until we discovered an area in the temple compound that was surrounded by a chain-link fence, behind which were hundreds of life-size Buddha statues. We found an unlocked gate and went in, hiding ourselves among the Buddhas. We knelt down to pray, with our foreheads to the ground, Buddhist style, for a long period in silence. We forgot about where we were.

When we finally stood up, a little unsteady on our feet, I saw through the Buddha statues a group of soldiers approaching the gate. Among them was a neatly dressed officer, obviously of some rank. They came through the gate and headed straight for us. My heart started beating wildly. "It's all over now," I thought. No chance of escape... Visions of being locked in a dark cell, no one knowing where we were — pain, death, worse...

I stepped in front of Rabia as they came near, trying to play the hero, my World War II movie script still running. The officer came directly up to me, his hand extended in a fist, but palm up. I backed up a little but he kept coming, now pointing to his closed hand and nodding, the other soldiers nodding too.

He opened his fist and inside was a folded *kyat* note, a currency worth less than a penny. Oh, I thought, having experienced this before, this guy's trying to sell me a black-market ruby folded in that note. I shook my head but they all gestured that I should see. The officer unfolded the note. Inside was a small green amulet, a little statue of the Buddha. He dropped it in my hand.

Then the soldiers and the officer smiled shyly and backed away, bowing to us with their palms together in a sign of respect and farewell, and without a word they vanished among the Buddhas.

Since then I have kept that amulet as a reminder of the ignorance inherent in my preconceptions. Sufis speak of this kind of ignorance as *taqyid*, "binding," in which our minds bind an experience to a preconceived idea, and then mistake that idea for what is.

I had bound my fear and my childhood war-movie associations with anyone looking like an Asian soldier. I thought I knew who these soldiers were, but my enemy turned out to be a warm-hearted human being who had seen two foreigners praying and kindly wished to express his respect for that simple act.

In how many situations and with how many people in my life have I repeated this kind of binding without ever being aware of it? What faces have I judged? What words, art, cultures, religions, philosophies, and even moments in wild nature have I blocked with a belief that I knew what was there before having actually experienced it?

When I track in myself the genesis of this binding of mental formations onto fresh experience, I see there is a contraction involved that arises from unease and insecurity. Something unknown in the present moment causes me to shrink into the limited space of a known thought-form.

How to loosen these bindings? For me the answer is clear, though not always easy to do. I must accept the underlying insecurity of the moment, and then open in spite of it. This opening is the key. It is always fresh, even startling, as if the world suddenly loses its borders.

My Sufi teacher, Fazal Inayat-Khan, echoed this same realization when he said:

We must come to the point at which we have the freedom, the courage, to look at things as a baby does, without foreknowledge; to let whatever new reality apperception comes, let it come in and experience it fully and totally, without understanding it. For understanding is only classifying something by previously established patterns of thought.

Be Still and Know

IMAGINE YOU ARE WALKING ALONE at night on a country road. No people or cars or houses around, just enough starlight to see your way, the only sound the sound of your shoes on the road and the swish of your clothes as you walk. You feel the stillness inside of things come close. You stop. Now there are no sounds, except the almost-never-heard hush of things being.

You sense the stillness on all sides and an identical stillness within you. It makes you uneasy, as if you are about to be extinguished. You try to think, to establish yourself against the stillness, but the voice of your thoughts sounds thin, metallic. You feel an irrepressible need to be distracted, to change the stillness and its overwhelming of you. You walk home, thinking about plans for tomorrow.

But in the quiet of your room you realize what happened: you got scared. You got scared of opening into the stillness, of allowing it to be. It was a close call. You see how throughout your life you have invited one distraction after another to prevent just this from happening. Now you feel disappointed in yourself. So instead of turning on your computer or reading a book or getting something to eat, you sit down and invite the stillness back.

A phrase you once heard comes to you, from Psalm 46: "Be still, and know." Be still. Be still.

You arrange your body as you have learned to do. You sit in a comfortable, alert position, with your back vertical so you don't slump or drift off. You let your body be motionless, quiet. The motionlessness of your body is a helpful friend; you know it is temporary, and in fact it is not really motionless — little shifts and sensations keep happening — but the relative stillness of your body reduces your identification with it, with the sense you are your body's ambitions and memories and likes and dislikes.

Learning to sit still, to settle like this, is called by Tibetan lamas "the first motionlessness." A quiet body at ease relaxes the persistence of thoughts. Once the first motionlessness has been learned, they say, then it doesn't matter if the body is motionless or moving, for then the ground of stillness is always available. But for now you need this helpful friend, and you sit still.

Now you invite what the lamas call "the second motionlessness." This is the still, empty openness "behind" each of your senses, the openness in which your senses arise. You relax into that openness. To say it is not moving points to its nature, but that's not entirely accurate. It is not the opposite of motion, or of the visible, or of sound. This motionlessness is not definable — it is not a sensation. Nevertheless it has an almost kinesthetic effect on you, as if it is vanishing you, as if the existing one you thought you were, the receiver, the photographic plate that records your experience, this "one," becomes transparent. You begin to feel the same threat of vanishing you felt on the road, but now you relax and let it be.

"The third motionlessness" comes now, unbidden. It is the stillness of presence itself — the stillness of a clearness that is always here, behind and within everything. It is what allows everything to show up. It is empty too, not made out of anything, yet it is awesome and radiant in its presence. *It is*, without being an *it*.

You remember now how the phrase from Psalm 46 continues: *"Be still, and know I am God."*

"God" — this old, strange word that sounds like a judge and yet still resonates beyond that — could it mean — could it have first meant — this empty Presence without form, appearing as all form? You realize you are trying to figure it out and you stop. *Be still, and know I am God.* The knowing is not thinking. It is presence being present to presence.

You find yourself wavering here — one moment at ease in the clarity, and in the next thinking about it. You hear the words again: *Be still. Do nothing. Let be. Don't fill anything in. No need to figure anything out. Relax.*

A sense of peacefulness opens in you, vast and without dimension. This is what Sufis call *sakina* — vast, peaceful tranquility without dimension — and suddenly you are smiling, your eyes are filling with tears — a joy — could it be called that? — a joyousness like praise and thankfulness together, love pouring forth from nowhere, the whole show showing up — mountains, sky, stars, bodies — from nothing, from stillness.

In remembering the Real, all hearts find joyous peace.
— Qur'an 13:28

Twenty-Three Suggestions for Entering a Solitary Retreat

1. Find a small cabin at the edge of the desert. Stock it with food and make yourself comfortable. Leave everything else behind. Now sit down and wait, knowing there is no right way to do this. Can you notice that everything that occurs shares the same presence you share? What is that?

2. Keep water in a bowl outside your window. The birds, deer, rabbits and chipmunks will acknowledge your consideration by drinking there.

3. Notice how the quietness swallows up each thought and breath, swallows even the movement of the tall grasses on the hillside.

4. Enjoy not having anything to do next. Trust that whatever needs to happen will happen when it needs to. Within the ease of that restraint, you are free.

5. You will probably review things — things from your life and thoughts about your future, or feelings that come up. Allow your reviewing thoughts to come and go like the birds landing at your water bowl. Nothing needs to be accomplished. Nothing needs to change. You don't have to figure anything out.

6. Gaze at the sky. Notice that its space extends through you. Experience your heart — the kind presence and volume of your chest — as spaciousness inseparable from the sky.

7. When you get hungry, wait. Pay attention to the exact sensations of hunger as if they are a new sound you are hearing. Listen.

8. Imagine the food you prepare and lift to your mouth is an offering made by the world to a holy one; when you eat it, imagine it is a sacrament of the holy world.

9. You may notice that whatever appears each moment has no continuity other than change. Crows fly from one side of your vision to the other. Like the events of last night's dream, things vividly appear but don't exist as they seemed to even a moment ago.

10. Consider that light is awareness itself. And let sound be the form light takes to be sensed by your ears. Consider that all of your senses are sensing forms of light, the delicious hum of presence.

11. Be vigilant about blame. Watch carefully how you might blame yourself for not doing something right, like sleeping late when you wanted to be with the dawn, or drifting off into an oblivious

thought-stream when you wanted to be clear and alert. Likewise recognize judgments of others when they arise in your mind. Watch how these thoughts, if you do nothing with them, evaporate in a continual forgiveness.

12. When you go for a walk, sometimes walk slower than usual. Let your eyes move and rest where they want to. The things you see — don't name them. Let them be just the light they are, the miraculous light of the world. Not tree, not bark, but just that light. Look down at your clothes, your skin. Consider that these too are light, not clothes, not skin. Now look to your awareness, the host of all this light. Consider that this too is light — the invisible light of awareness. Be light, be invisible light walking in light.

13. Be modest in your decisions about how things are. Watch the wren flit from twig to twig without deciding to or planning how to curl her feet around each davening branch. Who can know what is happening?

14. Will you pray? If you do, let your prayer be as gentle and as forthright as the sweep of your arm scattering ashes of a loved one from an ocean cliff.

15. Delight in the surface and texture of things: cup, cloth, stone, the shine of a spoon, the accommodation of a sock slipping on your foot, the liquid feel of water in your mouth.

16. Sit outside your cabin at night. Perhaps you will hear coyotes yip and sing under the inscrutable stars; perhaps, like them, you want to express your feelings to the night. Do so. No one's listening.

17. At night you may see in the distance a thin line of shimmering lights, the lights of a town spread along a highway twenty-five miles away. To you they are specks of light, but if your ability to see was magnified magically, you would see those specks are whole worlds of color, dimension, and presence: a child curled in bed reading a storybook, a man staring into his glass of beer, a leaf blown across the street. Consider that what you think you know is as partial as your view of the thin line of lights in the distance.

18. Do you want to change? Do you want this time of solitary retreat to result in a better you and a better life? Look carefully now. Can you find that aspect of you that needs improving? Where is the life that needs to be made better? Right now, what is missing?

19. Ask: what is this solitude? What is it to be alone? Is the changing cloud alone? Is the mountain? Are you?

20. Find silence. Stop producing sound. Notice that presence and silence are identical. Now, when a sound is heard, is silence lost? Is presence?

21. Dive often into the clear air of gratitude. No words are necessary. Just thank. You will know it by the slight upturning of the corners of your mouth, and an expansiveness in your heart, a pointless gladness.

22. Stop all effort. Relax without trying. Let the moment take over. Glide freely without making any conclusions.

23. When your retreat is over, don't go back. Welcome what comes, like the dawn welcomes what comes.

Three Men in a Cave

SOMETIME IN THE THIRD CENTURY C.E., a black Christian monk from Ethiopia wandered up into the desert region northwest of Damascus. This man, later known as St. Moses the Abyssinian, spent years with his followers praying in the caves that pocket these desert cliffs. One of the caves was lived in and prayed in by a succession of desert fathers. It became the focus for the sixth-century monastery built adjacent to it, now known as the Monastery of St. Moses the Abyssinian, Deir Mar Musa al-Habashi. A small group of us has come to visit this quiet place.

You have to bow down to enter the cave — it plunges like a tunnel into the mountain for about fifteen meters. Carpets have been laid on the floor, and a simple altar placed at its deep end. The silence in the cave is striking. In the darkness before dawn each day a few of us make our way into the cave to pray in that silence. On the final dawn of our visit, two men show up to join me. The darkness is lit by a single candle. I wait until they are settled on their cushions... and then I blow the candle out.

The darkness and the silence merge like lovers. We each begin to pray silently, stating with the voice of our hearts the reason we have come here. Then we are ready to begin the *remembrances,* simple words or phrases repeated many times, first aloud and then in silence. Their purpose is to open in our hearts an intimation of the One, the Only Being, the Ever-Present.

After some time we begin to chant a Christian prayer in Arabic, *"Ya Rab urham!"* which means something like: "Oh Rab (Nourisher, Teacher, Bestower of Existence)! Have mercy!"

"Ya Rab urham, ya Rab urham, ya Rab urham!" The words sound tender, comforting, intimate. They vanish in the silence. They re-emerge from inside us. They vanish again. With each repetition of the prayer a pulse of mercy radiates through us and vanishes in the darkness.

Mercy? What is this light that is like a warmth, and a sound, yet beyond sensation? We feel the familiar boundaries of our bodies become porous until the edges between us disappear, between us and the cave, and the mountain, and the light of the dawn outside. We sense the people awakening in their houses, the earth turning, the sun touching the land, everything happening at once, without boundaries, in a sea of mercy.

"Ya Rab urham!" we repeat, the sound of the prayer entering the silence of the cave like a heartbeat in a womb. *"Ya Rab urham!"* For a timeless moment it feels to us as if a new world is being created... and we are in the middle of its creation, in prayer in the middle of a mountain.

Praying in Death Valley

A LETTER TO MY FATHER (1994)

Dear Pop,

I write this from Death Valley in one of the most remote places I've ever been, on the fourth day of a solo fast. I feel quite weak, but peaceful. It is so quiet here. Time is nearly still – as still as my breathing. I have very few things with me – a sleeping bag, a tarp, some clothes. There are no distractions.

I think of the luxuriant green of your surroundings, the wind through a million leaves. I hope the hibiscus we planted survived after the cows got at them. I love the image of you chasing them off with a slingshot!

Here the valley and mountains are bare – just scattered creosote bushes on an undulating expanse of rock and sand. As my friend Meredith says, you sit on Grandmother's bones out here.

My little camp rests between two smooth hills that rise up on either side of me like breasts – I'm in the bosom of the earth. As I look up from this page, I see for miles across Death Valley to the Last Chance Mountains. This area is full of portentous names....

Why do I do this? Certainly not because it's fun (it isn't), though tomorrow, when I hike out of here, will be wonderful and joyous. The thought of a piece of good bread, or a strawberry! No, I do this for some reason that remains half-hidden from me, that keeps surprising me. I do it to burn up the dross that collects in my soul. I do it to burn up my forgetfulness and sloppy ways of living. I do it to remember simple gratitude. The ordeal of going without food or companionship or things to do is a surprisingly hard teacher – and an honest one.

I've been praying a lot out here. "Praying!?" I hear you say. I can imagine the idea of prayer may strike your Unitarian soul as superstitious or sentimental. And it's true, superstition and sentimentality are demons in the spiritual heart – I do my best to keep vigilant. Out here in this Big Quiet I rise in the first light before dawn and climb to the top of one of these hills, from where I can see for miles and miles. I do the same at sunset. And there I sing my prayers for a long time as the sun slowly rises or sets. I pray for the well-being of everybody and everything I can think of. I pray that your days will be many and filled with love, that your heart will be open and your mind free and your body strong. Simple things. I pray that all those who suffer will find peace and be comforted, that all those with vicious intent will be blessed with mercy, that all the hands about to commit violence toward another will be stayed. I pray for all my loved ones and family and friends. I pray that my life will be an offering to grace the beauty of the world.

And to whom do I pray? Who listens? No one. The God I pray

to is unknown to me. I know that any conception I have of God is not God. Of course I address this unknown God with many names: *Oh Gracious One! Oh Spirit of All! Oh Earth beneath my feet! Oh Loving Sun! Oh Moon and Mountain and Water of Life! Oh sweet Spirit of the Air! Oh you billion stars! Oh All Those who have come before me! Oh Generous Heart that beats through the world in ways known and unknown! Oh Great Mystery!* and many more....

These names of the Nameless open up the ground I stand on and the air I breathe and the light we all share, and suddenly Everything is Listening! Rock, lizard, crow, cloud – everything listens! I feel as if I partake in the Great Kindness of the universe – my prayers melt me into that.

Do you remember what Einstein asked, what he called the most fundamental question: "Is the universe benign?" I agree that the question is fundamental, but the answer is easy. To me the universe is so obviously "good" – though ruthless and indifferent at the same time. I believe that what we have emerged from, and what we will return to, is the indescribable essence of Blessing. This is not to say that I can turn away from or trivialize the world's suffering – whoever does that trivializes themselves – but even in the face of suffering, even in the midst of my own, a kind of Unfathomable Tenderness holds us, an Unbounded Grace – although these words – *Tenderness and Grace* – are only distant approximations of what is.

How did such an old humanist/atheist like you spawn such a wide-eyed pantheist like me? Actually, I suspect beneath the exterior you're a wide-eyed pantheist yourself. Maybe come Judgment Day we all will be.

I came upon the remains of a wild burro down in the wash the other day. Mostly bones – she had been picked pretty clean. Her skull was grinning, as all skulls do. What's the joke I wonder? Rumi said at the very moment of our death we wake up laughing. That little burro did.

Just before I started this letter I was sitting here gazing out at the Quiet and you came to my mind. I thought of your eighty-two years and that very likely, though not for sure, you will die before me, and suddenly I was filled with a great pang of missing you. I haven't written anything since I've been out here – it's too distracting – but that pang made me get out my pen and paper.

The idea of a world without you in it makes me lonely, though who knows, you might be dead even as I write this, or I might be as you read this. We live mostly in an illusion of our own projection. And maybe that is the magic of prayer and its power: it calls us to dive deep into what matters most to us, to find it, acknowledge it, and bring it up into the air. That's why singing my prayers aloud in my sing-song chanting way up on this hill with no one listening fills me with such love and gratefulness. An illusion of my own projection, which becomes truth. Like existence itself bursting out of emptiness, we mimic that incomprehensible act in our own little ways.

But what do you think? Is there a purpose or a meaning to all of this, or is it senseless? I wonder if the answer might be neither, or someplace between meaning and meaninglessness. It's like that beautiful painting you did years ago of a hand lifted up and open to the cosmos – all we have is the gesture. Meaning falls away, and meaninglessness falls away, in the beauty and thoroughness of each momentary gesture. And that's how I believe in prayer – it's a gesture, an offering flung up into the wind and blown away, an act of creation with no grasping for the results. "So be it," I sing, "So be it! Oh bless them and heal them and love them and make the way open before them in beauty! So be it!" And then? Only the Quiet remains, taking the prayers within it like invisible seeds, and I am left not quite who I was, no different from anything else, though so very me.

My subjectivity loses its edges out here. I remember reading somewhere that Jacob Boehme said, "Whatever the self describes, describes the self." And so this projection, this gesture of prayer, describes us. It is a chance to unfold ourselves through what matters most to us – like great music and art and dance and poetry. But then, all of our gestures carry this potential of prayer within them – a handshake, a kiss, making a meal, making love, wishing each other good morning, good night, have a nice day, be well! Prayers to the heart we share, and the Silence that holds us so tenderly. And yet, for all this high-minded talk of prayer, it's really not so special – in fact, it's quite ordinary. It's simply what we give. Prayer is what we give. We give thanks, we give love, we give support, we give respect, we give solace, we give compassion. Prayer is our gift back.

Well, maybe that's not always true – there are the prayers I sing for myself and those are gifts to myself.... "Oh Dear Heart, bless me with strength and responsiveness, free me from self-pity, teach me graciousness when I am self-centered, make of my life a worthy offering...." But look, there it is again, the gifting. We seek to rise above our heaviness and self-preoccupation. Why? To give and live more authentically, to love each other beyond conditions.

That's why I come out here, and why I guide others to come, because in some mysterious ways it completes the circle, allowing me to touch without distraction all that I care for and value, and to offer my life to that.

Of course it's also uncomfortable, and boring, and lonely – the wind blows incessantly or it rains for days or you can't keep your mind off food – but in the end you know it is the ordeal itself that transforms you. Strange, isn't it? Tomorrow, when I'm finally back in the world of towns and traffic, I'm going to find a strawberry and eat it slowly – and may I never again forget the blessing of that taste!

Well, I hope all this talk of prayer hasn't put you off. The demon of sentimentality lives off words – so often when we try to express the Ineffable it turns into pap. That's why I love singing my prayers all alone out here – the words matter so much less than the spirit they carry. Writing them down like this is much more treacherous. Perhaps a higher way would be to learn how to pray without words. Can we do that?

In the end I think prayer simply calls from us our deepest sincerity about what we love. When it does that, it escapes superstition and sentimentality and heals our isolation.

In this spirit I pray your days will be gentle and fulfilling and your nights full of peace.

…but now the wind is up, blowing sand in my face, telling me Enough Words! So may the Silence bless you.

Love,
Elias

With Hafez in Iran

IN THE DESERT CITY OF YAZD, central Iran, I start asking around to meet a Sufi. Having asked this kind of question before in a number of Muslim countries, I know it doesn't always work as I hope, so I add, "A wise Sufi who knows and loves Hafez, if there is someone like that here." After a day, word comes back there is one old man someone heard of, a simple holy man — perhaps arrangements can be made for me to meet him.

Later that night my young translator, Reza, and I find our way down a dark lane and turn under an even darker archway. We see a crack of light coming from under a door. We knock for a long time until an old woman comes. Beckoning us to follow her, she crosses a large unlit courtyard with stars overhead, through another doorway and down some stairs to a small room of mud-brick walls, books stacked on shelves on two sides, a refrigerator, a single mat on the floor, and a small charcoal brazier with a tea kettle bubbling on it. Sitting on the mat twinkling up at me is an unkempt man who looks like an ancient Walt Whitman, wild white beard and shoulder-length hair, eyes gleeful and sad at the same time. He gestures for me to sit on the one cushion facing him. Reza sits beside us.

Introductions are made. His first name is Shams-ud-Din. Reza explains that I am a Sufi from the west and we have come because we heard he was a Sufi. "No!" he says, "I'm just an old man. I don't know anything."

"Good!" I say, "I don't either!" and we laugh, pulling each other's white hair. (Later he admits to being a Nimatulahi Sufi.) It doesn't take long for Shams to become animated, quoting Hafez in great cadences and making gestures with his hands, stopping in mid-air to make a point and then continuing, punctuating his words with little gaps of silence. Although Reza does his best to translate, the conversation becomes less and less about what is being said and more about our delight in the presence of something invisible that begins to break through the humble earthen room, as if a seam in the surface of things has been peeled back, revealing a diamond-like brilliance beneath. I tell him this, pretending to peel back the old carpet we are sitting on, and the skin of his arm, and then squinting in the brightness. Shams laughs and sways on his cushion, reciting a couplet from an old Sufi poet about the same wondrous, hidden light. He plays the ney (flute) for me, and we speak of *fana* (self-vanishing) and *baqa* (abiding in emptiness). I ask him, "Do you still seek?" He says no. I ask, "So you have found God?" He says, "I have found myself."

I quote the hadith: "He who knows himself knows his Lord," and as we speak it seems the light inside things indeed breaks forth — I feel a warmth of pure benevolence glowing in everything. Almost giddy, we lean into each other like old friends, sharing the simple communion of mystic recognition across ages and cultures and languages.

Time passes — we recite poetry, joke, make little castles of words about God and knock them over, and then, before we leave he asks me, "So you have no religion?" I respond, "As Muhyiddin Ibn 'Arabi says, 'My creed is love.'" He takes hold of my hand, suddenly serious, and says, "God's shadow fell on you to lead you here." He accompanies us across the starlit courtyard, and at the door we say prayers for each other's long life, bidding each other *"Khoda hafez"* — God protect you.

What Needs to Be Done?

IN NONDUAL TEACHINGS WE OFTEN hear the pointing-out instruction that nothing needs to be done, that everything is perfect just as it is. While this is true from the ultimate recognition that everything occurs in the heart of God (so to speak), we may be puzzled by what it means in the relative world where there are things to be done, and where everything is not perfect.

The next election may turn out badly — that's not perfect; a vast extinction of species is resulting from human expansion — that's not perfect; cruelty and oppression occur every moment from Afghanistan to Kansas — that's not perfect. Clearly there is work to be done! So are the nondual teachings just some transcendent philosophy with no relevance or guidance for our struggling world? My experience is they *are* relevant — precisely relevant — though easily misunderstood. Their intention is to blow away our usual way of thinking about things, especially the idea that we are independent agents of change.

Some days ago I was in a supermarket, walking past the bakery section with all the cakes and decorated sweets arrayed in a big glass case. A mother was standing there with her little daughter who was maybe five or six years old. The baker behind the counter looked over at the little girl and asked, "Would you like to have this cupcake as a sample?" The girl looked up at her mother, who nodded it was OK. Suddenly the little girl clasped her hands together and twirled around, her pink dress like a parasol. As she came to rest she looked up at me and in a flash our eyes met. We both smiled, two strangers who had never seen each other before. Then she turned back to the baker and I walked on.

Did any of this need to be done? Not at all! The baker's question, the mother's nod, the twirling of the little girl, our smiles, all happened without need and without anybody doing anything. It was the instantaneous offering of the moment.

The nondual teachings that say "everything is perfect and nothing needs to be done" are pointing to precisely this suchness. They are saying we can have complete trust in what arises, including our spontaneous responses. We don't need to insert the idea of ourselves as agents of change into the situation — that's extra. This doesn't mean we don't bother to vote or help our neighbors. The instruction "nothing needs to be done" doesn't stop action, it just reminds us we don't have to separate ourselves from what is happening, or think that we need to instigate what is happening.

We're not in charge here. The little girl spins and smiles. Our eyes meet. Nobody does anything. We walk to the voting place and cast our ballot. Nobody does anything. It's time to wash the dishes. Nobody does anything. There's no one "in here" who causes actions to happen independent of everything else that's happening.

An endless stream of appearances flows by and vanishes, including our own actions in response to this stream. Everything is this flow.

We need not draw back and worry about what this means or what we should or shouldn't do. We can completely trust the moment to guide us. But even to say that may be misleading – there is no guide in the moment – it just happens the way it does. So let it! When our responses spontaneously occur in the moment, free from the conceit that we are their cause, they are naturally loving. They are not our responses anyway. The whole show is happening all together, all at once, and in its essence it is made of unconditional love. If challenges come to our well-being — which of course they will — then we need only be present in the moment, responding naturally without "doing" resistance or anxious concern. The stream keeps flowing without our trying to manipulate it.

A friend who read the above paragraphs challenged the sweetness of the story about the little girl and the cupcakes and parasols. "What if," he asked, "you were buying a newspaper at a 7-11 in a rough part of Chicago, and the strung-out mother in line ahead of you slapped her little girl in the face for asking for a Twinkie, slapped her so hard that the little girl fell to the ground... And as she picked herself up off the floor, your eyes met... what then? What would not-doing look like in this case?"

My response is there is no telling what it would look like. Perhaps you would begin to sing. Perhaps you would offer the girl your hand to help her up. Perhaps you would look at the mother and say, "I wish I could lighten your load." Perhaps you would begin to cry. Perhaps you would put yourself between the little girl and the mother. Perhaps you would suddenly, spontaneously place yourself in danger in order to protect a little girl you had never met before.

The point is there is no recipe. *When we do nothing, the love we are made of does the doing.* The little girl in the bakery spins around and we smile without thinking. The little girl in the 7-11 looks up with tears in her eyes and we sing, or give a hand, or cry without thinking, with complete trust in the response that comes. "Not-doing" is the absence of effort. "Not-doing" is natural ease. You recognize you are not subject to the strain of believing you are a doer. You let what happens happen, all of it, including your effortless response. When there is no effort, love acts.

The Gesture

EARLY ONE MORNING YOU MIGHT repeat to yourself, very slowly, a self-guided meditation something like this:

> *Open now into the clear presence of this moment.*
> *Let it happen by itself; no effort is needed.*
> *The clear presence of this moment is already so.*
> *It is at peace, silent and open.*
> *The transparent awareness that I am now is primordial*
> *and all-pervasive. It is this moment.*
> *Thoughts cannot encompass it, so relax.*
> *There is nothing I need to do.*
> *Nothing needs to change by my choice,*
> *nothing needs to be improved by my will.*
> *Relax. Notice that the mind makes up little stories,*
> *and then they vanish. No need to believe them,*
> *just let them appear and vanish, as they do.*
> *I am this clearing in which they arise and vanish, untouched.*

This is my natural state.
Relax. Nothing needs to be done.

Then, after a while, you might find yourself getting up from your meditation and returning to your daily agenda. Perhaps you make some breakfast and while you sip your coffee or tea, you read the paper. There you are reminded that countries are at war with each other; people are being killed and maimed; corporations and their wealthy owners are becoming richer and more powerful as ordinary citizens struggle to keep up while the poor sink deeper into hopelessness; old people die lonely deaths; the oceans are full of trash; the polar caps are melting; a massive extinction of life forms is occurring; and politicians are squabbling about nonsense.

You look up from your paper and gaze out the window. How is it that "nothing needs to be done" when so much in the world is crying out to be done? Shouldn't you try to respond to what is crying out to be done? You've heard spiritual teachers say that you must start with yourself, that you must first make peace in your own heart before you try to make peace in the world. You've heard it said that the phenomenal world is somehow illusory anyway, and that striving to change it is, in one teacher's words, "just pushing around the pieces of samsara to no effect." You've also heard it said that since the "Absolute" is perfect, and since nothing is outside of the Absolute, nothing needs to change. And even if you did try to change the world in some way, what difference would your tiny effort make in the enormous storm of ignorance and confusion that is raging everywhere?

Many times, in the arc of my own life, I have come face to face with questions like these, and with the dilemmas they seem to present. But I think there's a misunderstanding here, a mixing of categories and vocabulary. Yes, peace begins in my own heart, and yes, all phenomena *are* an expression of the perfect, luminous ground of being. But this truth is evidence of the seamlessness of my being with all being. If I start with an intention to do good and approach the suffering of the world with the attitude that I'm going to fix it, that good intention just gets in the way. It's extra. It builds a conceptual illusion that "I" am the cause of an action, as well as the one who can determine its outcome. As Krishna famously said to Arjuna in the *Bhagavad Gita, "Do what you do, but dedicate the fruits of your actions to Me."* This means release all attachment to the fruits of your actions. Don't even be concerned with them; they are not your business.

The cry of the world is still there — it's everywhere — and you are seamless with it. There is an old person living alone just a few houses from yours who hasn't smiled in weeks; there is your own son or daughter or father or mother with whom you haven't been fully present; there are refugees from the Congo in your city who need to learn your language; there are people on the other side of the world who have no idea of the freedom you enjoy and the creativity they are capable of.

Of course you can't respond to all of it. You can only respond to what is yours to do—what comes to you to do. And that doing is not about doing good or accomplishing a preconceived plan. Yes, there may be plans and goals, but they are ever-changing targets set up by our minds. They are not where the action is. For example, say you are the leader of the U.N. and you set the goal of ending world hunger; the action is not in that idea but in the millions of little moments when people actually show up and contribute to creating a sustainable human-earth ecology. Or say you are in a relationship and you express the wish to have a happy, fulfilling life together; the action is not in that idea but in the thousands of little moments when you actually show up and contribute to that happiness.

Each one of those moments is a gesture, pure in itself because it is not burdened with any notions of self-importance or pre-conceived ideas about fixing anything. It is a pure gesture because it arises from your natural seamlessness with the world—either the world far away or the world close at hand. In my own life I have been surprised to find myself responding to the cries of the world far from my home culture in places I had no idea I would ever go: Burma, Palestine, Iraq, Iran, Syria, Pakistan, Afghanistan and a dozen other places, and in every instance what kept the action true was not the outward goal of whatever service I was involved in, but the simple purity of the gesture itself.

A gesture is something free. It arises naturally from the situation and your caring presence. It is always spontaneous, like a smile or the tones of a song. After the 9/11 attacks, I felt, along with millions of others, the world breaking into ever-greater fear and distrust. I realized I could respond, not because I thought I could change the course of history — the fruits of my actions are not my business — but simply because I *could* respond. My wife and I traveled to Iraq before the U.S. invasion and made friends with the Iraqi people; I spoke at Friday Prayers in Damascus to a mosque full of Muslims and reflected to them their own generosity of spirit; with the help of many friends we painted great prayer flags in Arabic and stretched them across a desert canyon in Syria. The point wasn't to accomplish a particular goal, but simply to make these gestures in a spirit of friendship as best as we could.

You can't help but respond to the cries of the world — even your non-response is a response. If the baby is crying you can ignore her, or get irritated, or get anxious and fuss, or sing to her. So how do you know what to do — with the baby, or with the old person who hasn't smiled, or with the distrust between Muslims and non-Muslims? You don't. It was only when I was in Iraq or Pakistan or Syria that the gestures most appropriate to each situation showed themselves in the moment. If you're a detached observer or some kind of opinionated authority, you will only make matters worse. It is when you are intimately present with the baby that you will know what to do.

Your spontaneous gesture is born from your intimacy with life. Since it arises from the awareness of your seamlessness with all being, it is naturally caring. It is simply kind without the thought of being kind. And it brings life to a situation — a smile to the old person down the street, comfort to the baby, a moment of trust with strangers — because it is not a plan or an intention or a goal. It isn't what you do that makes a difference, but the love inside what you do. And for that love to be present, nothing needs to be done. It comes by itself, revealing the way forward.

For the Sake of Others

THE STORY GOES THAT IN CERTAIN Native American tribes, when a person became psychologically unstable, she or he was placed in the middle of a circle of tribal members — men and women, children and old people — and required to spin around and around until collapsing to the ground. The tribal member toward whom her body faced now became her special charge. She was obligated to care for that person, see to their needs, and be their companion and friend. The understanding was that caring for someone else is what stirs personal healing.

When we ache from the pain of loss or rejection, the pain of depression or loneliness, the pain of feeling unloved, from bodily pain or even the pain of impending death, the ache can feel agonizingly private to us. We feel alone in our pain: it encloses us in an isolation that feels terribly unfair. How is it possible then to offer care for others?

When Robert Kennedy lay dying from an assassin's bullet, his blood spreading across a kitchen floor, he opened his eyes and asked,

"Is everyone all right?" I like to believe that question eased his homecoming. At least it taught me this counter-intuitive calculus: *when you are in need, give.*

Giving in this way requires a shift in our hearts. In moving from self-concern to other-concern, we enter a deeper belonging.

The Native American ritual is charged by the healing power of belonging, not altruism, for altruistic behavior benefits another at one's own expense. The circle of tribal members embraces the wounded person, who returns that embrace. Both are healed.

So to say "when you are in need, give," is not an injunction to be virtuous or to sacrifice your need in favor of another's. It is to step from the loneliness of separation into the seamlessness of Being where nothing and no one has ever been separate from anything else. Our absolute belonging is not an idea, nor do we need to make it happen, nor make ourselves worthy of it. It's already and always so.

"Stepping into the seamlessness of Being" doesn't require us to travel any distance — it may be more accurate to say it steps into us when we allow it to. A generous heart is first of all a receptive heart.

If I feel the need to be seen and loved for what I am, and if I sit in that need waiting for someone to respond with what I need, I might sit for a long time in disappointment. But if I stop waiting and simply give, as best I can, what I've been waiting for, my world turns inside out. The connection I longed for is revealed — maybe not in the way I wanted or expected, but in a more fundamental sense of belonging. I am now able to receive.

The way this happens is a kind of magic that is always available to us. The distressed woman falls to the ground. When she looks up she sees in front of her an old toothless grandmother. She gets to her feet and approaches the old woman. She takes her hand. What is it that passes between their hands?

Speaking of
More or Less

You are my favorite person.
My sister is prettier than I am, but I'm smarter.
November is the worst month of the year.
If I had more money I'd be happier.
You are the least considerate person I've ever met.
The Prophet Mohammed is the greatest prophet.
My mother loves my brother much more than me.
The French are less friendly than the Italians.
Christianity is the one true way.
Who is the most fun person you know?
I like broccoli much better than Brussels sprouts.

THE HABITS OF COMPARATIVE MIND are pervasive, showing up in our characters and in our cultures, influencing the quality of our moment-to-moment experience and situating us in a shifting, tricky world of hierarchy-making in which the value of things is judged and rated. As the list above shows, comparative mind is thoroughly common to the ways we think and express ourselves, so much so that we might well protest that comparing things is an essential tool for making the world intelligible.

And it is, to an extent. We need to know when the water for the baby's bath is warm enough, or which shirt looks better for this occasion. But these two examples reveal a practical, direct use for making comparisons, and the comparisons are limited to the immediate situation: the shirt to the occasion, the water temperature to the baby. They do not assert categorical judgments.

In one of Robert Hass's poems, he paraphrases the seventeenth-century Japanese haiku poet Basho:

Basho said: avoid adjectives of scale, you will love the world more and desire it less.

Oddly, the power of these words is not weakened by their own paradoxical use of adjectives of scale — loving *more,* desiring *less.* It almost makes fun of itself, revealing how persistent and functional the logic of comparison is. Basho warns us that when we compare, when we set up distinctions of greater or lesser value, we pull ourselves back from direct intimacy with the world and join instead the restless range of desire. We insist broccoli is better than Brussels sprouts, judge our mother's love in terms of quantity, consign November to the lowest month in the scale of months, and assert that someone is the funniest, or the least considerate, or the most favorite in relation to everyone else. The world as we experience it becomes heavy with the accretions of our value judgments and competition, and we are left desiring all those things, people, or feelings that happen to land at the upper end of our scale.

Desire in this sense means I want this and not that, I like this better than that, I wish I were higher on this scale of value, etc. Thinking like this divides the world into hierarchies of preferences, subtly, and not so subtly, distancing us from what is. Basho is telling us how to be of the mind of haiku: just the thing itself, the thing on its own terms, the taste of Brussels sprouts as it is, the prettiness of my sister as it is, no comparisons necessary. It is what it is.

When we live and speak that way — avoiding adjectives of scale — we don't entangle our judgments into our experience of things; we relax the imperative of liking and disliking what arises. What arises is just what arises, and we can respond to it directly. We allow it to be itself: the taste, the mother, the month, the moment of feeling hectic, the person we honor.

And in that way, without rating it, counting it, or judging it, the world comes close. It is what it is. Then we can desire it less, and love it more.

Spiritual Communion

ZEN MASTER DAININ KATAGIRI once said, "Spiritual communion is the true meaning of emptiness."

How could that be? The idea of spiritual communion sounds comforting — the essence of true love — while the idea of emptiness doesn't sound comforting at all. Recently someone told me of a woman who quit her Buddhist meditation practice because it was too nondual, meaning it kept draining away her sense of self, leaving an empty void where before there was the richness of being the particular person she was. "I want to be a *me!*" she protested.

We can sympathize, can't we? This sense of me-ness is our most familiar refuge, our home base. From it we judge whether the world we meet is friendly or not. My *me* is what plans to make things better; it has ambitions and picks and chooses what it likes and doesn't like. As a refuge, my *me* is private, a private space I can open up or close down according to how safe I feel. When I feel very safe I can say to another person's private space, "I love you." This feels like communion, a connection — however fragile — between my me-space and yours. "I love you" also implies future safety and pleasure: you will be safe and happy with me in the future because I love you.

But as we have all probably found out, most of the "I love you" messages we have given or received in our lives have had a limited shelf life. The person we were so in love with at age twenty-two may no longer be someone we love.

So what's the deal here? Is love — the spiritual communion we experience — an impermanent transaction between two *me's?* Or do we perhaps have this confused?

If you look carefully into the nature of your "me" — how it actually is — you see that it has no solidity. You can check this out right now: looking directly into your sense of self — how it is to be your "me" — you can't help but come up empty-handed. That's because "me" is an idea, not a thing. Your "me" is empty of everything, including "me-ness." This is not to say we don't have a recurring sense of "me-ness," only that when we look into that sense, it's empty.

The problem many people have with the notion of emptiness — that it is blank, juice-less, love-less, etc., — arises because they imagine emptiness to be something. It isn't. Emptiness is empty of itself. Emptiness is empty of anything we might think is emptiness. It can't be held in a definition because it has no edge by which to define it. And yet it shows up as this sense of me! My *me* is empty of me-ness and it is also empty of being empty.

People studying nonduality often claim they have no self, and that there is no such thing as a self. But what is it they don't have? A self! How could we speak about "self" if we didn't have some sense of what we're signifying with that word? Could it be that I neither have a self nor don't have a self, just as emptiness is neither empty nor not empty? That is, it's empty of being empty?

This kind of word-play can leave us frustrated, or it can reveal a gap in our thought narrative. The trick here is not to land in an assertion — i.e., "I have no self" — but to open into the gap created by the double negation: I neither have a self nor don't have a self. If you sense that gap, allow yourself to fall into it. Open into it, open into openness, and glide.

Openness is another word for emptiness. What I describe as the "open path," accessible to all of us, is a contradiction in terms, since the path that is open is empty of pathness — it's not definable in that way. As we learn to not define but open into openness, into emptiness, we recognize that this "emptiness" is what knits everything together. It's the ineffable presence that is the nature of your "me" and my "me," and the nature of everything we ever thought was solid or existent.

This is how spiritual communion is the true meaning of emptiness: everything is empty of thingness, and therefore everything is seamless: one, whole, all at once. Recognizing this directly, not intellectually or abstractly but as a living reality, is so joyful and relieving because you realize that love — spiritual communion itself — is not subject to temporary feelings but is the shoreless ocean we swim in.

The emptiness we feared would annul us and wipe out our chance to be in touch, to be in spiritual communion with each other and this beautiful world, turns out to be exactly what makes everything present to everything else, the one in the many and the many in the one.

The Way It Is

RIDING MY BIKE THIS MORNING — blessed moment! — the world turned inside out. I saw that what I thought was happening wasn't happening the way I thought it was. I thought I was riding my bike, that the sun was shining on me and the street, that the blue sky was above me, that people were driving their cars past me, and that it was ten after nine in the morning. I thought everything was normal, the way I thought normal was: blue sky above, sun above, street down here, car over there, bike and me moving from where I was to where I was about to be.

But suddenly — how I don't really know — I saw it wasn't actually that way at all, that Shakespeare was mistaken when he said that "all the world's a stage" and we are mere players upon it, with our entrances and our exits. It just seems that way; we think it's that way, while the mystery of what's actually happening is hiding right in front of us, like space.

I was holding the handlebar of my bike with one hand, a roll of blueprints I had just picked up from the printer with the other. My feet were turning the pedals. The sound of tires on pavement entered my ears, a breeze touched my face. And then all these parts of the world, all these objects and phenomena and sensations — so apparently separate from each other and interacting with one another — showed me their indivisibility: *nothing is happening independently from anything else: it is all one piece, all light, an infinite field of light-forms appearing from "stillness" and vanishing into "stillness" with no more claim to continuous substantial existence than the images of last night's dream.* The sun was not up there shining down on me here. I was not a person in space, on a stage entering and exiting. I was not a separate something in a universe of somethings.

The entire assemblage of the cosmos, all the seemingly individual events occurring in this instant now, spontaneously arriving and instantly changing, revealed to me that they are nothing other than the same emerging empty presence, the same empty presence that *is* all this light and sound — the caress of breeze on my face, your eyes moving along these words — none of it happening in time but simply all at once, appearing like the splash of a pelican diving into water, the bird already gone, the drops of water glinting in the sun, the splash already gone.

I saw that there was no time in which I could be a "person," that the idea of personhood is simply an idea, already gone like the pelican's splash, and that all that is, is just this unstoppable, spontaneously emerging now — the same empty presence instantaneously displaying itself in all these myriad ways without ever once becoming them — and that I am and you are this same "light" without substance, this transparent light that appears as everything.

I didn't think of any of this — it was simply and suddenly evident from my unity with the common identity of everything, with the way it is. It was evident, too, how these beautiful bodies and the dramas of our lives are the fleeting forms of empty presence: simply how it is dancing now, dreaming us up, playing as light.

We are of the nature of light, appearing out of clarity. The nature of this "light" is bliss, a numinous, holy joy. This may seem like a big step — to associate light with supernal joy — and it is only persuasive when experienced directly, not thought about. But when we do get it, we see that the whole human drama is not as serious as we thought it was. No one is doomed. No one will miss their reward.

Reward? Yes, but not a reward we'll collect later. Our reward is already given: the good news at the heart of reality. The good news is: everything is all right forever and ever. We are of the nature of light, the most beautiful joyous presence we could ever possibly imagine, and beyond that too. But if we don't get this now because the seeming separation of things into distinct entities is too convincing, no matter; we will most certainly remember at the moment of our death.

I began laughing out loud as I rode along, and a college girl passing me in her car smiled and waved, seeing I was happy, but how could I tell her that the joke I was laughing at was the joke of all jokes: how we think we are something separate that could die, how we think we're going somewhere, when in fact we are the whole thing — there's nowhere to go! We have never "existed" as something separate, as a substantial entity, and we never will.

But even telling it like this somehow misses the main point — the most obvious fact — which is that this moment is alive! You can feel its aliveness in the presence of this instant, the way it invisibly blooms as everything. After all, life is not just the province of carbon-based organisms — life is how emptiness shows up as form and timelessness appears as time. This dimensionless, ever-emergent moment is alive! And it is Life without an opposite, without the illusion of death. Seeing this, Sufis gave God the name: *Al-Hayy,* the Alive.

But the Aliveness that is "God" doesn't exist in any location, separate from everything. It is the Aliveness of now.

The way it is, is Alive. You and I: Alive. Even when we exhale our final breath and our heads drop down: Alive. But of course, there is no you and no I, no breath, no life, no death, no numinous holy joy, no reward, just this ultimate, spontaneous Aliveness that leaves no trace, evident in the togetherness of all that is.

Loaves and Fishes

I WENT TO MASS THE OTHER DAY at the small desert chapel near my home. As I walked along the dirt road leading to the chapel I noticed a bluebird hopping along the edge of the road. As I passed she flew, but she only managed to clear a sagebrush and then landed again. It looked like she had a broken wing. I felt helpless, knowing it would just make matters worse if I tried to catch her. *Well, maybe she'll be okay,* I hoped, and went on to the chapel.

In his homily, Father Eric recounted the story of the miracle of the loaves and fishes, how there were all these hungry people — thousands of them — following Jesus around, but there was no food available. Jesus had just heard of the murder of his friend, John the Baptist, and was grieving. But the peoples' hunger touched him — both their spiritual and physical hunger — and he asked his disciples to find a solution. The disciple Philip was a can-do sort of guy, Father Eric said, but even he couldn't come up with a solution — except to send the people away, which would be like sweeping the problem under the rug, ignoring both of their hungers.

But then a small boy pulled on Jesus' sleeve and offered him five little loaves of barley bread and two sardines. We know the boy was poor because barley bread was the staple of the poor — the better-off people ate wheat. These were small loaves that could fit into the palm of your hand. We remember what happened next — Jesus took the bread and fish and miraculously fed the multitudes with it.

That was a miracle for sure. But there was a prior miracle: the moment the boy tugged on Jesus' sleeve. His offering wasn't a solution to the problem, but it was the best he could do. I imagine the look on the child's face, lifting up the hunks of bread to Jesus. Right there, that's the miracle, in that gesture. The boy knew he couldn't solve the problem, but that didn't matter. He offered what he had from the innocence of his heart.

After Mass was over and I started walking back home, I suddenly understood it. In our time each of us is facing "the hunger of the multitudes": the slaughters, wars, suicide bombers, refugees, climate change, soil loss, species loss, racism, injustice, inequality, despair. We are facing problems of such magnitude and complexity that we naturally shrink back from them like the disciples — denying them or avoiding them. After all, what can we do? It seems like there are no solutions — at least not solutions that we have the power to make happen.

But we do have our version of little barley loaves and sardines. What is it? What is it we have to give?

Our care.

Caring may not change anything; it may not assuage anyone's hunger or avert any disaster, but it's what we have. This little tenderness of our hearts, this caring, this willingness to be touched by the world's suffering — we can offer this. Every act of caring, no matter how small, frees us from self-absorption and disconnection, and acknowledges our interdependence.

Some theologians have suggested that Jesus didn't actually multiply the number of loaves and fishes. They say that when people saw the little boy's gesture, they were overcome with shame, for they had been hiding food in their robes. When the boy gave his food away, they all brought out the food they had been hiding, sharing it until everyone had enough. That's a miracle too. One child's caring ignited everyone else's.

What our care produces in the world isn't really our business — we don't care in order to produce an effect. We just care. Our caring will show up however it does — in acts of kindness, understanding, generosity, patience, protest, resilience, creativity. In the end, acts like these may not save the world, but at least they'll grace it.

As I walked back from the chapel I came to the place where I had seen the bluebird, and there in the middle of the road was her dead body, squashed by one of the cars leaving the service. No one's fault. And yet the great juggernaut of human heaviness was what rode over her, just like it is riding over the delicate world, just like it killed John the Baptist, just like it hid the loaves under peoples' robes. What can we offer in the face of that heaviness?

I picked up her body and took it into the desert away from the road, said a little prayer and buried her. It wasn't much; it wasn't a miracle. But it was what I could do.

No Teacher,
No Student,
No Path

As I grow older I seem to be spending more and more of my time in the role of "spiritual teacher." I teach courses and workshops, lead retreats, write books and essays, and counsel many people. It's a valid role, to be sure, but at the same time it seems to be a role built on a series of mirages. The whole business rests on several assumptions that may be temporarily useful, but are not actually true in themselves.

For one thing, there is the idea of the teacher and the student. The teacher, it is assumed, has something the student does not. The student is in some way incomplete, lacking the knowledge and insight that the teacher has in greater supply. This unequal dynamic is indisputable in most other areas of life: the piano teacher knows more and has greater skill than her student, the professor of mathematics has more knowledge and a wider range of mathematical imagination than does his class. But in the realm of spiritual realization, is the teacher really more "advanced" than the student?

As we know, spiritual realization is not a matter of accumulating more facts, knowledge, or skills. If anything, it is characterized by non-effort and non-doing: learning to stop learning, learning to stop trying to acquire anything. This "stopping" is the heart of the matter. The whole idea of acquisition of spiritual insight, of attaining enlightenment, implies the odd notion of possession. "Does the dog have buddha nature?" asks the famous koan. The enigmatic answer, "Mu!" which more or less means "No!" is not aimed at answering the question but at puncturing its assumption that buddha nature is something that can be possessed.

If the dog, or any of us for that matter, cannot "have" buddha nature, then how can we understand this? What is this buddha nature, this realization of the essence of things, this enlightenment? Does the teacher have buddha nature? Does the student? Does the Buddha?

Enlightenment is simply not attainable. No one "has" it and no one can get it or give it. The truth, what Sufis call *al-Haqq,* is not something that comes in portions, with some capable of having more of it than others. *Al-Haqq* is ubiquitous. The One – the Real, Primordial Nature, Rigpa, the Clear Light – is not something hidden or waiting somewhere else. No teacher, not even Jesus or the Buddha or Mohammed or Guru Nanak, has or could have any more of it than anyone else. It isn't "haveable."

This is what I mean by the mirage of teacher-student inequality in the process of spiritual education. It's simply not how it functions. The clear light of pure and total awareness is this moment. No one has or could have more access to it. The mirage of inequality between the spiritual teacher and his or her students in this regard may have some provisional utility in keeping students around long enough so they stop making up stories about enlightenment, but that provisional utility is still provisional. It is still a mirage.

Teachers who don't make this clear to their students do them a disservice, as well as run the risk of self-inflation and creating dependencies and spiritual hierarchies. This is a subtle matter. Teachers who approach it directly and sensitively can free their students from dreamy patriarchal stories, saving them much heartache. At the same time, students can benefit from being aware of these same dynamics, even if the teacher is not.

Another mirage in the process of spiritual education is the idea of the path itself. The path, the quest, the spiritual search, is an image that — like the teacher having something the student doesn't — implies that what is sought is not here now, but will be discovered when the path is traversed and its destination is achieved. But there is no path to anywhere. There is nowhere to go. The destination is already here, and can only be found by not seeking it. This, too, is a subtle matter. As Al-Bistami, a ninth-century Sufi, said:

This thing we tell of can never be found by seeking, yet only seekers find it.

The same message was echoed by Shabkar Lama, a nineteenth-century Tibetan master:

Looking for it, the vision cannot be seen: cease your search. It cannot be discovered through meditation, so abandon your trance states and mental images. It cannot be accomplished by anything you do, so give up your attempt to treat the world as magical illusion. It cannot be found by seeking, so abandon all hope of results.

The idea of an incremental spiritual path, with degrees of attainment or "stations" as Sufis call them, can serve as a carrot to keep the seeker present to the work at hand, but it can also be misleading. The geometry of a path, with a here where "it" isn't and a there where "it" is, is simply not possible. Enlightenment only happens now. In fact, it is now. Anticipating that enlightenment will happen in a future now ensures it will be missed.

Of course, we have the sense that the truth is hidden from us, even if it isn't. It is "hidden by its oneness," Ibn 'Arabi tells us. Because it is utterly present, always, it is transparent to our faculty of discrimination. What shows up instead are all the constant discriminations we make: this thing, that thing, this thought, that thought, this feeling, that feeling, inside-outside, self-other. These discriminations crowd into every moment of our waking lives and monopolize our attention. What they emerge from or within — the clear light of now — is looked through but not recognized.

To the extent that we are caught up by our discriminations (judgments, points of view, beliefs, etc.), the idea of a path does have provisional utility, like the teacher-student distinction. But this kind of path is a path of dis-illusion, de-construction, or "un-learning" as Sufis call it. Notice that these words (dis-illusion, etc.) all point to the same aspect of stopping, of relaxing the grip of believing our thoughts. The path in this sense is a kind of anti-path, a path not of attaining knowledge about a belief system but the opposite: a path of unknowing. "O Lord," cries Mohammed, "increase my perplexity concerning You!" which means: free me from all conclusion-making!

The final mirage is a mirage endemic to most spiritual teaching. It is the famous distinction made between the archetypes of the absolute and the relative, God and everything else, the sacred and the profane, unconditioned pure awareness and the conditioned realm of manifestation. Defining these polarities can help us initially to allow that there may be more to heaven and earth "than dreamt of in our philosophies." In this way they may work as provisional pedagogical devices, like pointing out a previously unseen pattern in one of those figure-ground optical illusions.

The problem here is that our minds quickly reify these archetypes. We think they actually *are* something. But the Real does not come in pieces. It spontaneously occurs, all at once, and leaves no trace. Emptiness and form are not two separate dimensions. The unconditioned and the conditioned don't happen in different places. It's true they are not the same, but neither are they different.

The teacher, after necessarily pointing out the One that seems to underlie the Many, has to put Humpty Dumpty back together again. Not One, not two. There is no conclusion about *what is* that can be made. The only thing the teacher can really do is help students cultivate the ability to hang out in this unknowability and indefiniteness — whether of mirages like the teacher-student inequality, or the path, or the seeming polarity of the One and the Many — and partner them as a friend in mutual enchantment with the Mystery as we live it.

The Practice of Openness of Heart

EACH OF US IS CARRYING AROUND a priceless treasure — our openheartedness. Although it is often covered by our thoughts and agitation, the openness of our heart is always there, waiting underneath; it can't be diminished or destroyed. There is nothing more important in life than uncovering our heart quality, our openheartedness. It's what allows the world to touch us, and what allows us to touch the world. If we feel life has betrayed us, if we feel life is not really worth living, or that we ourselves are not worthy, it is because our natural openheartedness has been covered over.

We can't grasp this heart quality with our intellect; we can't understand it, but we can free it. Freeing it takes practice, because our judgments and disappointments about our lives can be so stubborn. How can we take on this practice?

Heart opening usually happens without our intention — it just happens. We all know this in the "love moments" of our lives, when we spontaneously feel the preciousness of another being or of a situation. A baby looks up at us as it crawls on the carpet — the baby, the look, the sounds from the kitchen — all of it suddenly precious and fleeting and sacred. Our openheartedness in that moment is freed. But moments like this are all too rare, and we must learn to invite them into our lives by gently practicing openness of heart.

One simple way to do this is to follow three "movements" that can be described as *calming, opening,* and *blessing.* In order to practice openness of heart, it helps to be calm. Calming the body, sitting still, stopping for a moment the flow of our activity, breathing quietly, letting our thoughts pass by without obsessing about them — these are the familiar methods of meditation that help support our calmness. When we are calm, our whole being comes together in its natural presence.

Then, calmly, we can turn our attention to our chest area. This is where we can first sense our heart quality. It's not the physical beating heart, but something intangible, something very subtle and tender and alight. At first we may not experience anything identifiable, just a slight spacious feeling. If we relax right there — and this is where calmness helps — the second movement of our practice begins: *opening.* We allow that small, spacious feeling in the center of our chest to have the full share of our attention. We open to it. As we open to it, we notice that it, too, is opening. It doesn't stay in our chest but expands like an invisible light into the clarity of our mind, our sight, our hearing, and into the totality of our perception.

This sense of openness is subtle, and we can easily look past it for something juicier and more tangible. But once we realize that it isn't tangible, that it is openness itself, we become comfortable with its subtle nature, and we can allow it to saturate our whole being in its gentle quality. It feels good, but what we're feeling is not like other feelings. It is goodness without an object. It's a kind of warmth, but not a warmth of temperature. It's like a radiance without any source, a radiance that fills our inner life and our outer life simultaneously. That is the heart quality, pure openness of heart. We could also call it warm-heartedness, or kindheartedness. Although it is subtle in itself, it is the very power that will save the world, and continually does. In the storms of selfishness and violence that have devastated human history, this delicate heart quality is the very thing that has guided our ancestors and allowed us to survive. It reveals to us what truly matters, and what is worthy of our care.

The final movement of our heart practice — *blessing* — comes by itself, though we can learn to direct it in specific ways. When our heart has opened this profoundly, we can imagine that we are able to gather, for a moment, this intangible light, this warmth, this kindness, into a singular current that streams out of our chest toward a particular person, or a group, or a situation in the world. For a moment — and it doesn't have to be long, perhaps as long as a kiss — we imagine this current of blessing flooding into and around that person or situation. It blesses.

Notice that when practicing openness of heart in this way, the practice relies upon our feelings and images of embodiment: our calm body, calm breathing, calm mind; our chest and the small spacious feeling there; openness flooding through us; a current of light streaming out in blessing. These images give form to what is formless. After a while, when we are well practiced, these images can soften, and even fall away. Then our practice of openness of heart becomes like a song without words.

Nondual Sufism

"NONDUALISM" AND "NONDUAL AWARENESS" are names that refer to direct recognition of the clear light of timeless awareness that is the matrix of all apparent existence. This clear light is beyond being; it cannot be known as an object of knowledge or named accurately, though it is ever present. Direct recognition of the clear light does not belong exclusively to any tradition or spiritual view. It is our common inheritance. When we speak of a nondual Buddhism, or nondual Christianity, nondual Vedanta, or nondual Sufism, we are referring to particular styles of revelation and expression of this common inheritance.

We in the West typically think of the Sufi "style" as heart-centered — Sufism as the way of the heart. But this is only part of the story. Sufism is often marked by poetic expressions of warmth, friendliness, and intimacy, but Sufism can equally be experienced as penetrating, relentless, and dissident. So any descriptions of a Sufi style are provisional. I like to think of its style of nondual expression as spontaneous rather than predetermined, subversive rather than safe. It does not stay within a particular pattern. Indeed, the expressions of nondual Sufism range from silent contemplation of Divine Absence to ecstatic celebration of its Presence.

Sufic nondualism is animated by a flow of aliveness that resists crystallizing into a system of thought or belief — although it does not hesitate to enjoy thought and belief for the delight or communion they may reveal.

As a style of awakening, nondual Sufism is open, free-wheeling, inclusive in view and practice, non-definitive, experiential, non-sectarian, warm-hearted, and non-attached. It embraces the full range of human experience while settling nowhere, capable of a subtle openness and freedom from attachment that is equally open to spontaneous delight and sensual extravagance. Expressions of nondual Sufism are grateful for beauty in all its forms of disclosure, recognizing happiness and grief and all emotions in between as free offerings of the Unnamable into Itself.

Nondual Sufism is simultaneously a way of negation and a way of affirmation: it negates conclusion-making while affirming the indefinable. A kind of love-mysticism, it loves the edginess and poignancy of human life while seeing through its apparency to the stillness within.

Present without agenda, kind without being moralistic, it reaches across the seeming divisions between people and societies with the confidence of the light that is common to us all. Nondefinitive and unpredictable, the transmission of nondual Sufism is guided by silence — and by the intimate wisdom arising from the unity of embodiment and emptiness.

The Eros of Nonduality

MY FATHER, BLESS HIM, TOOK A number of psychedelic journeys in his life, beginning back when the use of LSD was not illegal. He was looking for the direct experience of "truth," uncomplicated by religious interpretations. He took great care to make the "set and setting," as he called it, of these journeys peaceful, beautiful, and conducive to inner exploration.

When he was in his late seventies, he came to visit me in California. During that visit he took one of his last LSD trips after a gap of more than a decade. I'm telling this story because of something he said — just three memorable words — as he stood in my back door-way, having taken a dose of LSD. He was looking out at the backyard garden. He stood there watching the branches of the trees swaying in the off-shore breeze, the sunlight shimmering in the canopy of leaves, the blueness of the sky and its invisible contact with the textures of the earth. He took a deep breath and happily exclaimed, "It's all sex!"

As he tried to explain to me later, what he meant was not only that everything was in intimate contact with everything else — not only were the earth and sky, the trees and grass and flowers, the sunlight and moisture, all in a grand and continuous copulation with each other, which in that moment he was witnessing — but that (and here he struggled to express himself) time and the timeless, the apparent things of this world and the no-thingness of the silent, empty ground of being, were somehow generating each other. They were exulting in an embrace so passionate that the entire cosmos could appear and yet not be fixed in time or space, but be ever becoming.

I don't believe my father's vision of the fundamental eros of reality was a hallucination. I think he touched, in that moment, the joyousness of all being/non-being, God's joy. As Rumi describes it:

> *God's joy moves from unmarked box to unmarked box,*
> *from cell to cell. As rainwater, down into flowerbed.*
> *As roses, up from ground.*
> *Now it looks like a plate of rice and fish,*
> *now a cliff covered with vines,*
> *now a horse being saddled.*
> *It hides within these,*
> *till one day it cracks them open.*

My father died alone in his sleep several years ago. He doesn't exist anymore as the human being he was. I want to resist the easy consolation of saying that he still lives in my love for him, or in the gift of this little story. He simply doesn't exist anymore. What does exist — without existing as anything solid — is the universal eros he realized, the joy of roses, up from ground.

As it says in the Quran somewhere: *"Everything is perishing except*

His Face." God's Face — the Uncreated Light — shines as this unspeakable joy of creation without end, the spontaneous exuberance of atoms humming everywhere, and in this, as this, we appear and vanish, like my father has — momentary sparkles of infinite love.

Seeing the One World
with Two Eyes

EVEN THOUGH THE ESSENTIAL NATURE of reality is nondual (literally "not two," not divisible), we humans experience the world with the two eyes of duality. This is because we have the ability to conceptualize. Even to say the word "nondual" is to conceive dualistically. When we say "nondual," our minds are already at work, setting up the "nondual" here and "duality" over there.

Perceiving dualistically is not a fault — it's the way we've been made. If I say the word "I" it means I have conceived of myself as a subject. This is natural enough, isn't it? "I" wake up in the morning, "I" brush my teeth, "I" love you, and so on. It is a convenient way to think, even if it isn't exactly how things really are. Phenomena actually arise not as subjects and objects, but as a whole, all at once. Because we see with the two eyes of duality, however, it's not easy for us to see the wholeness of things.

The ability to distinguish between "this" and "that" makes it possible for us to navigate the world. But if we cannot also see through the utility of dualistic thinking to the nondual nature of reality that is ever-present and all-pervading, we limit our lives in ways that cause illusion, conflict, and suffering.

A Zen master once remarked, "We must learn to realize nonduality through duality." Is this possible? Can we use the two eyes of duality to see the one world of nonduality? That is to say, can we realize the truth of nonduality without devaluing or "transcending" the nature of form? Can we understand what Sufis mean when they say, "Nothing matters *and* everything matters?" Can we grieve the loss of a loved one even while we know nothing is lost?

In nondual teachings we often find phrases like: "everything is perfect as it is," or "nothing ever happened," or "this is all a magical display." Statements like these, while true, seem to deny what we also know to be true: that everything is *not* perfect as it is, that something *is* happening, and that, magical display or not, this world is beautifully, heart-breakingly real.

I once held the hand of a young woman as she died. She was wide awake when the moment came. One could say that nothing actually happened at that moment — it was like the space inside a jar "meeting" the space outside when the jar breaks — nothing really happened — and yet something clearly changed.

There is no way to resolve this paradox by thinking about it. Only the heart can encompass it, and the heart doesn't think. "To see the one world with two eyes" (Rumi's phrase), we have to allow the heart to see through those eyes. The seeing heart is like a musical instrument that lets the song be played but doesn't cling to any melody. The ephemeral beauty of our lives, the love, the losses, the injustice and cruelty we witness — the only way we can bear all this without turning from it, or hardening ourselves, or becoming overwhelmed, is to bear it in the open tenderness of our heart.

And what is that? What is the heart? Again, we have to stop conceptualizing. The heart we call our own is not ours. We might say it's God's heart, or the heart of the All-Good, or the heart of the Totality. It's the heart inside of things. Through it flows all the experiences of beauty and praise as well as all the grief and despair that has ever been and ever will be. The heart I am trying to point to is not a private thing. It's vast, boundless. It bears all. It sees the one world because it *is* the one world. It doesn't limit or exclude anything. As Jack Kerouac tells us:

> *Not in thoughts of your mind*
> *but in the believing sweetness of your heart,*
> *you snap the link and open the golden door*
> *and disappear into the bright room, the everlasting*
> *ecstasy, eternal Now.*

Beginnings

I ONCE ASKED THE POET COLEMAN BARKS for a prayer to be included in our anthology, *Prayers for a Thousand Years*, a prayer to honor the beginning of the third millennium. Could he offer something that would invoke the spirit of the millennial turn?

In response he wrote a poem about a little boy in a restaurant who, bored with the grown-ups' talk, stood on his chair, *"holding the railing of the chairback as though to address a courtroom."* The boy looked around and then declared in a loud voice, *"Nobody knows what's going to happen next."*

Perhaps this is the thrill of beginnings: when we let ourselves not know what will happen next, then anything can happen — the new might really be new, innocent of our previous behavior and conclusions. From this new beginning we might truly be happier; who knows? The possibility thrills us, and from sheer good-heartedness we wish fresh beginnings for everyone: *Have a good day! Good morning! Good evening! Happy New Year!*

Imagine how often beginnings come — they are endless! We

close our eyes each night and begin to sleep, not knowing what dreams will stir in us. We wake each morning to begin another unwritten day. Not expecting things to be the way they were, we can be like artists at the moment brush touches canvas — completely given over to beginning. We are probably more pleasant to be with too, not finishing each other's sentences, just simply and intimately sharing the unforeseen present without preconception.

And what about this common, ordinary moment? Is it too a beginning, or is it what follows after? Is what follows after not also a beginning? The new infant takes its first breath and a human life begins; the priest says, "I now pronounce you husband and wife" and a marriage begins; a loved one dies and grieving begins. Each micro-slice of now permits the unknown to follow after. The great nouns — birth, marriage, death — are nothing other than verbs; they never really exist in themselves; they are fluent melodies, unfixed, improvised.

We ask: can I fall through time like this, always a baby, always a man or woman surfing the curl of the wave, nothing preconceived? Don't I need to, and want to, plan ahead?

Of course! But planning too is a beginning, and surprise is available at every moment if we only allow it. We make our grocery list, and then banter with the grocer, making him smile. Not on the list! We follow the planned pattern for the dress we're sewing, the scissors in our hand turning curves just so, adjusting, adjusting, experiencing the living responsiveness that is the heart of work. This moment has never happened before!

If we think we know what will happen next, boredom drains the life from us. If we don't think we know, we join the all-pervasive, spontaneous light that illuminates everything from the inside out, this and each timeless instant.

What we call "plans" don't get in the way; they are part of the flooding light too. It is only when we wallpaper the world in front of us with our plans that we are reduced to living inside that stuffy decorated room. And it's not just our plans that wallpaper the light; all our self-talk, self-concern, and self-positioning papers over with the little habits of our minds the light that comes from nowhere.

But the wallpaper is never impenetrable – with a sigh or a smile we are out!

Even now, the never-ending dawn is circling the earth, refreshing our little planet without pause. It shows us how to begin.

Summertime Reverie

THE PAGES OF SUMMER ARE TURNING now, like a big children's book with large print telling simpler stories than winter did — the pages falling lazily open, almost by themselves. They show quiet dawns with only birds around, then breakfasts and plans being made... then stories of wonderment and fear fill the noons and afternoons, stories that end always back home, at evening, with stars in a sky painted aquamarine... and then we sleep.

We dream. We dream slow, roiling dreams of how all this has come to be, how over millions of seasons and days we were made from light and the stuff of stones and water, how we were fashioned into plants and animals, into canopies of leaves swaying, into small paws on the forest floor, and then a sudden click of stick, our ears go up, and then a pounce and we change form, again and again, all of it changing, all of it given, the sun given to warm us, the earth given to hold us, the dream given for us to see *we are the given,* given here as the merest drop of sperm and egg, given to grow in the womb of our mother, given there the same as we are given now, given now the same as the moment we were lifted from our mother and given to her breast, given to be beings like this, walking on two feet, the planet looking out of our eyes, us upright, free moving, vertical with voice above heart above belly above knees above feet, unrooted from the planet but given from it, everything, all of it, given!

We wake, still half dreaming, and ask, "What has given all this?" But almost as soon as we ask we know that in trying to answer we'll be just making something up, *for this that gives is hidden in the given and can't be taken out.*

"But is something asked of us?" we wonder. "We've been given everything! Everything! For what? Is something asked of us?"

Lightly we fall asleep again and dream these words:

Miraculous Beings! You are given to give! You are given to give! Give thanks! Give praise! Give love! Give warmth! Give forgiveness! Give kindness! Give!

We wake again and see a new page falling open on a summer morning.

Doing the Beautiful

A FEW SUMMERS AGO I WAS SITTING with the renowned potter Alan Caiger-Smith, out behind his fifteenth-century house in the English countryside. Alan's garden was brimming with life — pole beans were winding their way up a trellis, chickens were pecking under the apple trees, honeybees were looking for blossoms.

"I had a lovely experience last week," he told me as we drank tea. "It happened right here on this bench. I found a little bird in the grass, a fledgling. It couldn't fly. It must have fallen from one of the nests under the eaves. I put it in an upside-down basket so the dog wouldn't bother it, and tried to feed it a mosquito and water from my palm."

I looked at his hands. They were over eighty years old — long, wide fingers splayed from decades of turning pottery on the wheel, yet delicate too. Alan is famous for his glazes, for the confidence and sensitivity of his brush-strokes, and especially for his mastery of "luster" — the iridescent shine achieved through careful adjustments in the firing process.

"The next day," he continued, "the baby bird was looking poorly. I thought it might be cold so I put it in my hands to warm it." He made a closed cup with his hands to show me. I imagined the little bird in there, warming in the dark inside those leathery hands, little cracks of sunlight appearing along his fingers.

"Then I opened my hands to see how it was doing. And this was the amazing thing. It looked at me and then all of a sudden it flew up and swooped around the house and was gone! It had never flown before! I felt so honored to be present, like a mother, at this little being's first flight."

Sufis speak about *ihsan,* which is often translated as "good deeds." *Ihsan* literally means *"doing the beautiful,"* as in Rumi's famous line, *"let the beauty you love be what you do."*

Alan had organized his life around doing the beautiful. Shaping each bowl and vase by following the beauty of their lines as he coaxed them up from lumps of spinning clay; sensing the faint changes of pressure and glide on the hairs of his brush as the liquid glaze and curving forms spoke back to him; and most mysterious of all: his being called by the beauty of the not-yet-visible luster, the shimmering light that seems to illuminate the glazes from within.

Like the little bird flying up from his hands, the beauty Alan loves reveals itself spontaneously. Perhaps this is what doing the beautiful means: spontaneously responding with complete freshness, unencumbered by effort of any kind. And perhaps in "beautiful doing" there's no "doer" or "doing" at all — just the potter's hands, the spinning clay, the unmoving center, the beautiful form, all occurring spontaneously and without interference.

Medicine Beauty

WHEN I WAS A TEENAGER MY FATHER said to me, "Your life will feel meaningless unless you contribute something, unless you leave the world a little better, a little more beautiful, than when you found it."

Perhaps because he was an artist and a philosopher, I interpreted this father-to-son guidance as a lesson in aesthetics as well as ethics — that is, *how well we live depends both on doing good and on doing the beautiful*. Gradually, over the years of my life, I've come to see how every beautifully made object or place is a positive contribution to society, just as every beautiful thought, every beautiful gesture, every beautiful work, in fact, every experience of beauty makes a positive difference. As Dostoyevsky famously said, "Beauty will save the world."

If this is true, then we have a hint about how to live a meaningful and beneficial life — a life that fulfills not only our own needs but also reduces suffering and makes a wider happiness possible.

What is beauty? Is it simply "in the eye of the beholder?" If so, is all beauty relative? Or is there something about beauty that is true for all of us?

The most embracing definition I know of beauty is Ibn 'Arabi's: *"Beauty is the welcoming openness of the Truth toward us."* This definition lifts the notion of beauty out of the relative realm, out of the preferences of the beholder's eye. It suggests that something more profound than aesthetic appreciation is happening when we are touched by beauty.

But it's not easy to speak of this. As soon as we name beauty, it becomes a concept rather than an experience. With that in mind, I'd like to suggest here a few things I've come to sense are true about the *experience* of beauty — these are intuitions, not definitions — images of the ways the beautiful moves through the world and quietly saves it.

BEAUTY WELCOMES US.

Somehow beauty reaches out and greets us, even surprises us, as when we step out the door and see the morning light spilling across the lawns and streets, see the trees' leaves golden-green, their palms raised up, brushed with light. Or when the baby wakes up without fussing and you hear her making little noises in her room, cooing nonsense syllables — you are greeted and welcomed into an existing beauty that touches your heart.

BEAUTY ARISES IN OUR QUIETNESS.

We can't know beauty if our insides are noisy. When you experience something beautiful, you first need to pause, to stop at least for an instant and open a quiet space within you, to let the beautiful in. Between your thoughts, it is the space that listens.

BEAUTY IS LIFE–GIVING.

You can feel beauty's vitality directly. Not only does the experience of beauty bring the beautiful object, or place, or music to life, it enlivens the perceiver. The origin of this aliveness is one of beauty's most profound mysteries. And the beautiful gives away its affirmation of life democratically, to everyone equally, like the sky's beauty — its cosmic darkness, its high-piled clouds, its fresh breezes — the beautiful aliveness of the sky is for all, and free.

BEAUTY FITS.

A hill town in Umbria fits its landscape; the colors of the dawn fit with one another and with the moment; the unfolding notes of a symphony fit with what has preceded them. A response is beautiful when it fits the whole context. Ecologists describe an ecosystem's health by what they call *good fit* — for example, an oil spill doesn't fit in a delicate marine environment, just as a McDonald's doesn't fit in a beautiful village on a Greek island. Here we can feel how *good fitting* — beauty itself — is essential to the health of any living system.

BEAUTY IS KIND.

Isn't it true that the little acts of kindness that come out of you — the unplanned acts that appear spontaneously, that are generous in themselves, that expect nothing, no recompense, like when you make someone smile without any forethought on your part, or when you listen intently to someone who needs to have their feelings heard, or when you let someone move ahead of you in a line or in traffic — isn't it true that these little kindnesses are beautiful in themselves, to both you and the one who receives them? Kindness is beautiful.

BEAUTY REMEDIES INJUSTICE.

When relations among people are unjust there is discord, anger, and poor fitting. Although beauty is not something to be enacted like a recipe or a law, it can guide our intuitive moves toward remedying injustice — Mandela's forgiveness of his jailor is an example of how a beautiful act can heal. A society in which relations are fair among people, where the right to live and flourish is equally available to every being, is a beautiful one.

BEAUTY DECENTERS US.

When we open ourselves to the beautiful, we have to get out of the way to let it in. The experience of beauty destabilizes our sense that we are the center of the world. It subordinates us to a wonder that is larger than we are.

BEAUTY IS MORTAL.

To experience beauty we have to accept and share in its evanescence. We can't grasp the beautiful moments of our lives; they vanish, and as they do we feel the exquisite poignancy of our mortal lives.

BEAUTY LEAVES THANKFULNESS AS IT PASSES.

Gratitude may be beauty's sweetest gift to us, if we can receive it. The things in our lives we are most grateful for — are they not beautiful? Our breath. Our body. Our child. Our friend. Morning light. This moment.

The Abyss

TWENTY YEARS AGO I COLLAPSED in a Chinese restaurant in a
dusty town near Death Valley. I had just come in from a four-day
fast in the desert. Foolishly, I had eaten too much too quickly, plus
I had a rum drink — garnished with a paper umbrella — to celebrate
with the others. I stood up from the table, suddenly terribly dizzy,
and then crashed into the neighboring table of elderly blue-haired
ladies. I didn't know it then, but I was suffering from insulin shock,
a potentially lethal condition. I experienced the slow-motion
sequence of events reported by people in moments of violent change:
the world tilted, I heard the crash of plates, everything went dark;
yet I felt utterly calm, even indifferent, as the floor slowly gave way
and I fell, without stopping, into an abyss.

As I fell I began to forget. I didn't even care enough to remember
what was happening, who I was, or where I was. The whole meaning
system of my psyche was slipping away, and I didn't even care. The
stories that defined my life were vanishing, utterly and silently, like
a child's soap bubbles disappearing in the air,

I felt at peace, weightless, and aware without self-reference. I remember that feeling most of all, the feeling of objectless awareness, though it was not really a feeling. It was simply clear and pure presence, sufficient unto itself.

Then I heard a voice, very far away. The voice was calling a word, again and again. The word sounded familiar. Then I remembered: it was my name! The voice was calling my name. The smallest glint of desire began to form in me — though there was hardly any *me* left — just this little spark of desire to find that voice. What was it? Where was it?

Then suddenly there were more sounds, the voice became louder — it was my wife's voice calling my name as she knelt over me on the floor of the restaurant. A friend who was with us knew about this kind of situation and saw what was happening to me. She told my wife to keep calling my name, and gradually her call brought me back to a sickening, spinning world with harsh lights and sounds and a crowd of tall shapes bending over me.

By the next day I was fine again, just embarrassed by the spectacle I had caused. But the experience taught me something about the vestibule of death. It taught me that one day I will forget my own name, and my children's names, and the names of everybody I ever knew. I will forget what blue is, and sky, and the colors of this world. I will not remember the name of my country, I will not remember what a Sufi is. I will not remember any story about anything. And, I imagine, in that moment I will no longer be able to hear anything, so no voice will be heard, and no glint of desire will arise to find it. But none of this will matter. It will be perfectly all right to forget this beautiful world.

Coming empty handed, going empty handed — that is human.
When you are born, where do you come from?
When you die, where do you go?
Life is like a floating cloud which appears.
Death is like a floating cloud which disappears.
The floating cloud itself originally does not exist.
Life and death, coming and going, are also like that.
But there is one thing which always remains clear.
It is pure and clear, not depending on life and death.
What then is the one pure and clear thing?

— Zen Master Seung Sahn

Blessedness

I WENT TO VISIT YOU BEFORE YOU DIED, do you remember? I came to your little cottage for breakfast and we spent the day together. I brought croissants and orange juice. You made that delicious coffee. I remember how sunlight — blessed sunlight! — slanted through the window and spread across the breakfast table like a benediction. We knew you were dying, that the cancer was taking you fast, but you still had your plan to beat it with some kind of wavelength machine you had ordered. It hadn't come yet.

Our glasses of orange juice were golden in the sun. The croissants left little crumbs on our plates. All the trivial details that day felt important. You went into the back room, rummaged around and brought out a fur hat you said was your favorite. "Here," you said, "I want you to have this."

We took a long drive through the countryside and got lost twice. Do you remember that little stone bridge we stopped at? We spoke about the method they must have used to build its arch, a century or so in the past. We sat on the bank near it and tossed little twigs into the water as we talked.

I told you my vision about light and you really understood it. Now that you're dead — what an odd word! — you probably understand it better than I do. I pointed out how light rays (or waves, or whatever they are) obviously go in all directions because when we move our heads from here to here there's no interruption of the light rays coming from, for example, a little white pebble at the water's edge. And what was equally amazing — all the light rays from all the things we could see were passing through each other without bumping into any other light rays. The whole place was dense with constant light! You looked down at your hands and your clothes and said, "Look! I'm that way too!"

Then we speculated about the universe, how the light from all the stars was going in all directions all at once too, so that even as the earth zooms in its orbit around the sun we still can look up and see uninterrupted light from each single star — now from here and now from here, fifty miles away from where our eyes were a moment ago.

I remember that moment. You looked at me and said, "That means the whole universe is not dark at all, or even empty — it's filled with light, everywhere! It's solid light!" We were quiet then, taking that in.

That was when it happened, that sense we had of perfect meeting. Up to then we had been good friends, of course, but this was different. It was like suddenly we weren't there as two people, you and I, but as one "Here" without form, transparent to ourselves. There was a sense of clearness right through us and right through everything, and yet the forms of the water, and the bridge, and the trees, and our bodies were all still there, specific and vibrant.

We looked at each other again and I saw the tears on your cheeks.

It was unbearable, how that moment hurt. After another long silence watching the sun wavering in the water, I said to you these lines from Kerouac:

> *There is a blessedness surely to be believed, and that is that everything abides in eternal ecstasy, now and forever.*

You didn't say anything back. We helped each other up and walked back to the car in the sun. And then when I started the car you looked over and asked, "Where shall we go?" We both smiled a little, I think, and then I remember we leaned toward each other, restricted by our seat belts, and bonked foreheads. Thanks for that day. Thanks.

Death Song

I want to die with open eyes,
I want to see the wanting leave,
the ties come loose, the brilliance fade,
and shudder not, but lift away,
finished, peaceful, sad,
to enter endless fusion
with all this good, happy, true illusion.

Free Fall

PLUMMETING FROM SO GREAT A HEIGHT with no parachute, slowly cartwheeling, his body now facing upwards at the retreating sky, now downwards at the puffs of cloud-tops scattered across the patterned earth, it seemed to him he was not really falling but stretched out weightless, suspended in a space in which he had time to remember and rest. The furious beating of his heart moments before was now calm. He felt enveloped in an intimacy so close that no sense of peril could enter.

An image of his mother came to him from when he was a young child. She was looking down at him from her place by the stove, her kind eyes and smile. But instantly the image flashed away, leaving behind a swelling of light in which other pictures came: of him as an infant crying as the door closed, of the new tricycle with the red ribbon on its handlebar, of a scoop of white ice cream in the dirt.

Now it seemed the images he saw and the feelings he felt were the same, not two kinds of perceptions but something else, a sensual, emotive history of his life, a life no one else knew. Warmth, skin, the faces of women so close then dropping away, the longing, the disappointments, great flashes of happiness, his children in his arms . . . it was like a history of meaning read in a language of feeling that he no longer needed to protect himself from. It didn't matter, none of it mattered, and he felt in his suspended falling, for the first time, the relief of being free from care.

Now he was swept by something extraordinary, a feeling that burst forth as the particulars of his life were released, a feeling of such dearness that he spread his arms out as if to embrace everything all at once, and in that moment he began to fly.

It was not a flight he guided, as he had guided his plane before it broke apart. He flew now surrendered to a vacuum ahead of him, pulling him into itself, drawing him forward. Once again an awful fear lunged at him, tearing through his body.

Then it was quiet. The sound of the wind rushing in his ears stopped. A clarity as clear as space, perfect in itself, appeared in his being as if it had always been there, but had somehow gone unnoticed until now. The clarity was everywhere; but since it included him as well as everything else, he couldn't tell any difference between "everywhere" and "here." The clouds, the azure sky, the massive earth and his plummeting body were made of the same radiant clearness without reference, vast but without distance.

The sense of his approaching death turned inside out. There was no approach and no death. The story of his having once been born dissolved. Nothing had actually happened; he had never gone any-where. Opening into him was a great happiness that he somehow already knew, a joyous, perfect home — what was it? — a placeless Place so beautiful and so familiar he wondered how he could have forgotten its presence and utter truth. It was old — no — it was always, never having begun so never ending, a happiness at the heart of Being that revealed his life to be gossamer, a play of light in an empty room, an emanation of a great Kindness, and all that he had ever worried about, or wanted, or grieved over resolved itself in that Kindness, and with a silent shout of joy he met the Brilliant Ground.

Meditation on a
Winter Night

Who is here is what is there.
— Ibn 'Arabi

NOW, IN THE QUIET OF THE YEAR, the night comes close to earth. Peaceful, impersonal night. It touches your face with its coldness as you make your way through the snowy woods, it touches the tracks of a mouse in the snow, it surrounds the thin moon to the East and the dark branches of the trees. Night. Between the branches, your home galaxy glistens, a great banner of stars.

You stop. You stop making noise crunching through the snow. You stop the small concerns of your thoughts. You join the night in its stillness. You stand there alone, wondering, wondering what's happening and what you are. Your wondering has no words; it doesn't presume it knows anything. It doesn't look for an answer.

An owl swoops through the trees and pulls up, wings wide, stopping on a high branch. You watch its small dark shape, framed by stars. You are alone together.

The owl, the galaxy — you wonder how the galaxy turned itself into all this — into the owl and you and into the trees and the tracery of the mouse's footprints in the snow. You wonder how the galaxy flung all this out of itself, and how it keeps on turning into everything in this quiet moment as if it were a living being, an aliveness inside everything that doesn't stop becoming snow and branches and moments. You feel the intimacy of this happening, the galaxy turning now into the warmth of your body and the mist of your breathing.

Your wondering lands like the owl on the very edge of the moment. The woods are quiet. What is inside of you, your privacy, loses its boundary and opens into the trees and the dark air, opens into a presence so familiar you feel it is you without you, the same presence of galaxy and night and owl, a presence of everything in everything.

And then, for an instant, something unbearable shines forth. Unnamable, indescribable — only later do you call it Bliss or say it felt like the Original Bliss of creation, *ananda,* the ever-present undisclosed radiance of a Happiness so exquisite and kind it bequeaths everything everywhere and resolves everything everywhere — all loneliness, loss, suffering, and death resolved without erasure in its infinite wonder.

Suddenly the owl drops from its branch and vanishes in the darkness. Just as suddenly the unbearable epiphany vanishes and you are left, almost invisible, standing in the dark woods in the quiet of the year.

Clear Light and the
Beauty of the World

FOR THE MOMENT OF OUR DEATH, when the messages of our senses cease and the contents of our mind become transparent, *The Tibetan Book of the Dead* offers this instruction:

> *Remember the Clear Light, the pure Clear Light from which everything in the universe comes, to which everything in the universe returns; the original nature of your own mind… Let go into the Clear Light, trust it, merge with it. It is your own true nature, it is home.*

When I first read that passage as a young man, I was deeply moved and reassured — it assured me that the confusion and loneliness I felt as a twenty-two-year-old would vanish one day in that great, final homecoming. I didn't understand what this "Clear Light" was, but it didn't matter — the certainty of the voice in the *Book of the Dead* comforted me. The Clear Light would come.

In the meantime, I would just have to make the best of it. So in the years that followed — my twenties and thirties — I kept attempting to find or build some kind of substitute, metaphorical home in which I could belong during my exile here on earth.

I realize now that I had succumbed to the old polarity of my species: the sacred hereafter and the profane here, heaven and earth, light and dark. As far as I can understand it, this polarity has its genesis in our need to identify ourselves as individual beings separate from the other beings and objects of the world: me "in here" and all the rest "out there." The dominance of the "me in here" sets up the added polarity of my suffering and incompleteness here and now versus the promise of redemption and homecoming somewhere else in the future.

Of course, these kinds of polarities are understandable — we are two-legged organisms walking about, seemingly disconnected from the earth and sky, anxious about avoiding any dangers that might be lurking on our path. It appears we *are* separate beings.

It took me a few decades of spiritual practice and inquiry — not to mention the normal sufferings life provides — to realize that the nature of reality only appears to be split into these dualities. As one of my teachers, Murshida Sitara Brutnell, once cryptically said, *"There is no other."* This whole show is one magnificent Happening, one awesome Brilliance reflected in the infinite prisms of possibility. Which means that we — you and I right now, every humming atom of us, every thought and feeling, every movement — are inextricably part of this blossoming of spontaneous light.

Sufis call this *wahdat-al-wujud,* the Oneness of Existence. Nothing stands outside of its Oneness and Suchness — there is no other. The multiplicity of the phenomenal world is sometimes imaged by Sufis as a veil over the Absolute, though the veil and the Absolute are not seen as two different things; rather "the veil is the external epiphany of the Absolute." Or, as the fourteenth-century Persian Sufi Mahmud Shabistari wrote, *"The whole world of Being is the beams of the Absolute Light. The Absolute remains hidden because it is so clearly manifest."*

Which brings us back to the Tibetan notion of the Clear Light, surely the same as Shabistari's "Absolute Light." The Clear Light is not, as I had first thought, something waiting out there to welcome me when I die. It is present now, right here, both perceptible as all the apparent things and thoughts and feelings of this world, and as imperceptible, invisible, and transparent as the awareness in which these words appear to us right now. The light of awareness, the Clear Light, "the original nature of your own mind," all indicate this same light that can't be seen or located, though it is unmistakably, spontaneously present. "God's Light is in the heavens and the earth," says the Bible and the Quran. And the Quran adds, "Whichever way you turn, there is its presence."

When I die, I imagine one of my last feelings will be, "How beautiful!" I won't be referring to the beauty of where I'm going (I have no idea about that), but the beauty of where I've been, this astonishing earth, sky, and cosmos, this astonishing body and its capacity to know and love. As the mystic-philosopher Francois Cheng remarked, "The universe is not obliged to be beautiful, and yet it *is* beautiful." How extraordinary!

The mystery of the Clear Light and the mystery of the beauty of the universe have become the central contemplations of my life. *"Beauty* [I'm fond of repeating these words of Ibn 'Arabi] *is the welcoming openness of the truth toward us."* Somehow the "truth" of the unchanging Clear Light is revealed by ever-changing beauty. "God is beautiful and loves beauty," a hadith tells us. Spontaneous, ephemeral beauty — the beauty of a song, a kiss, a passing cloud, a glint of sunlight — each one a momentary revelation of the unborn Clear Light, our home.

Before I Die

Recently I sat on a bench in a park talking with a friend who had been given his final diagnosis. The wind was playing in the tops of the trees. People wandered by, enjoying the sun. He spoke slowly, his words dream-like, drifting in and out of fantasy. When we said goodbye I went home and tried to write down what he said, but most of it had vanished. Here are a few lines I can recall:

I'd like to get it right before I die
live without leaving a trace
put the world in order
tidy up

I'd like to tell all the girls they're loveable
and all the boys they're good
so they'd smile all the way down to their bones
at the simple fact of it

I'd like to bow back to those trees
swaying their crowns in the sunlight

I'd like to say something so wonderful
that everyone would stop
for a moment
surprised by the sudden remembrance
that they already know what this is all about
but forgot
light playing on the wave of emptiness
this All-Good, All-Bliss, Home

I'd like to tell my children
there's no need to worry or be sad
and they'd believe me
except of course for the sadness we can't bear anyway
the sadness of appearing and disappearing like this
so dear
with none of us able to adequately honor
the precious moment of love we love

Before I die I'd like to visit
everyone's most intimate space and tell them
everyone
every man woman child I have ever known
that they are the favorite, the special one, the best beloved

I'd like to take this great carpet of the world
in my two hands and give it a shake
send a wave through it that would shake free
the ugliness we've done to it

I don't know what will happen when I die
and I'm glad for that
what I do know is it will be more awesomely loving
and beautiful than I could ever imagine sitting here

That's my faith
I guess

Here I remember he became quiet, gazing into the sunlit foliage of the park in front of us. It felt like he wanted to say something more but didn't know how. A young mother walked by wheeling a pram, followed by a little boy trailing a stick in the gravel path. After they disappeared he spoke again.

No
it's not my faith
I'm sure of it
I'm as sure of it as I am of this moment
how it is

so kind
after all our worrying and hating
still so kind

In One Form
or Another

I ONCE CAUGHT A VERY LARGE FISH. As it appeared from the depths of the sea off the west coast of Canada I saw it was longer than my arm, and I knew I couldn't pull it into the kayak I was in — there wasn't room in there for both of us. The sky was gray and close; the wind had picked up, blowing spray in my face; the rise and fall of the sea made my little boat unstable. I tied the line onto the kayak so the fish would stay close to the boat, its green body swimming next to me while I paddled to the shore of a small, uninhabited island. When I landed I pulled the fish up onto the pebbled beach. It thrashed and quivered, lay still, then thrashed again and again. I took my hunting knife from its sheath on my belt and plunged the blade just behind the fish's head, severing its spine. At that moment I felt a surge of energy like an electric shock explode up my arm and into my body. Later that night my friends and I ate the fish, but in that moment, as the surge of energy entered my body, I felt I had absorbed its life force. It turned into me.

Yesterday I was making a soup. As I sliced the carrots I remembered that fish and its gift, and realized the carrots were doing the same thing. The carrots, like the fish in its sea, had led private lives in the dark earth somewhere, had been pulled out and now submitted themselves to my knife. There was no surge of electricity that I could feel as I chopped the carrots, but the gift was the same.

This world is constantly feeding us like that. Even this breath we are drawing in right now — the life-gift of plants — offers up its power to us, keeping the continuity of life happening. All of us are brimming with this accumulated life force given from countless sources — carrots and fish and air — plus vast gifts more intangible but no less vital, like the perseverance and ingenuity of our ancestors: hunter-gatherers, nomads, farmers, singers, builders, scientists, or the gifts of our mothers and fathers, and their mothers and fathers, and theirs, all the way back, the parents whose caring for their little ones ensured our coming into being. The life force we breathe and move with pours into us from all this like the current of a great luminous river.

We can feel this directly, and we can also feel how this luminous current doesn't stop inside us — it keeps flowing. What we have taken in, gives. This is happening right now, it doesn't stop. Whether we are aware of it or not, the light of aliveness pours forth *from* us just as it pours *into* us. The aliveness of our seeing, hearing, and touching, the aliveness of our warm hearts, all of it continues to illuminate the world around us just as we are illuminated by it.

Of course there are rocks and obstructions in this great current of aliveness. Meanness, abuse, selfishness, fear — none of us escape being wounded by these things, or wounding others. Our job is to learn to get out of the way, to let the luminous current flow through us and not obstruct it. This is not so easy, but we can do it.

One thing that helps is *remembering to bow* — to bow in acknowledgement and awe of this current of aliveness that creates and sustains our own aliveness. What a vast gift it is! The simple humbleness of our bow — not necessarily outwardly but inwardly — in recognition of the unimaginable offering of a universe that makes our existence in this moment possible… this is what helps us get out of the way. To be here, alive with this aliveness, and not to be in its way, is the best luck we could have.

Even in sickness or the decline that precedes our death, the current of life still flows in its full vitality, if we get out of its way. Then it is not so much a physical vitality as a luminous one. For within this current of livingness that we are made of is an unquenchable light. It is the invisible light of becoming — so close we can't see it — that ignites the whole drama of fish and farmers, fathers and mothers. But now the metaphor of a "current" or a "river" comes to its limit, because this gift of aliveness is not limited by river banks — it is more like a shoreless ocean of light, or what Inayat Khan describes as "the all-pervading life in space."

Light, life — these two words spiral around and into each other until we cannot distinguish the difference. Ultimately, and intimately, our livingness is light — we are made of light. And yet even that word — light — meets its limit, for this invisible light is not the opposite of darkness, nor is it located in one place and not in another. In the same way, "the all-pervading life in space" is not the opposite of death. Ultimately, and intimately, there is no death. The fish, the sea, the soup, the air, the ancestors, us — we are all radiances of this invisible and timeless light. Or as Jack Kerouac tells it: "We've been here forever, in one form or another." Bowing down, we know what he means.

Oh!

IMAGINE THIS SCENE... YOU'VE BEEN visiting a friend who has a cabin near a lake. It's 2 AM, and not being able to sleep, you wander down to the lake in the dark. No one is around. You walk to the end of the dock that extends out into the lake. Daring yourself, you take off your clothes and stand there in the blackness.

The night sky is cloud-covered and dark, no stars. Your body is dark and the water below is dark. The darkness is cool on your skin. You want to dive forward into the air and the dark water, but you are afraid. Even the feeling of your fear is dark.

As you hesitate there, your whole life seems to be compressed into this moment: the way it has felt all these years to be a self, your self, alone in the midst of what's out there and what comes next. It's been this way for as long as you can remember: the sense of being "you" in here, confronting the "it" out there.

The darkness becomes so intense you withdraw from it into the only safe place you know: your self. But now with a shock you feel your self is just as dark as everything around you. There's no safe place, no refuge. The darkness goes all the way through.

At that moment you give up. You stop caring about being safe or not being safe. What the hell... without planning or thinking, you dive into the darkness.

Suddenly the intensity of the darkness is overtaken by a silence that is even more intense. Your body, stretching forward in a perfect arc, is enwrapped in silence. For that brief moment suspended over the dark water, the passage of time stops. The silence reveals itself to be without beginning or end, or to have any duration. It goes right through you. You *are* silence.

And then the world erupts into a crashing, splashing roar of cold water, bubbles, and light flashes churning in the silence that doesn't move. The coincidence of timeless silence with the coitus of body and water snap the last thread of your old separateness, and as your head surfaces you shout, *"Oh!"*

★ ★ ★

Oh! is the best of our words. Nearly pre-verbal, nearly without meaning, it is the spontaneous sound of mystic surprise. It is the sound of humility and honor, of welcome, surrender and awe all at once. It is the sound of the naked soul opening into its home light. When Sufis invoke names sacred to them they say, *"Ya!"* which is their way of saying *Oh!: "Ya Hayy!"* — Oh Alive! — *"Ya Fatah!"* — Oh Openness! Or as Mechtild of Magdeburg sang in her prayers:

> *Oh burning mountain! Oh chosen sun!*
> *Oh perfect moon! Oh fathomless well!*
> *Oh unattainable height! Oh clearness beyond measure!*
> *Oh wisdom without end! Oh mercy without limit!*

It is a sound that fits great choirs of angels in their praise, and a sound that lovers tell no one else. At the moment of our death it may be our last sound. *Oh!*

Could *Oh!* also be our most intimate spiritual practice? Could we let it voice the surprise of our hearts as we wake in the morning, or turn a corner, or see the light in a passing face, or when we hear the news of a plane crash or a bomb going off and wish to offer something to the dying ones — *Oh!* This sound doesn't even have to be spoken, because before it is a sound it is silence as big as the sky — the silent, blissful, transparent now, ever surprising us with what we are.

Dark Lament

So much given, so few who know.
So much beauty, so little love.
— Wendell Berry

WHAT CAN WE SAY TO ONE ANOTHER to heal this wound of our regret, of having lived so many moments oblivious to their gift? We've had things to do, of course, and now we have more, the twitter of facebook pages leaving us breathless, but can we say we are here the way the rain is here or the way the deer looks up from the grass?

Our cities press against the ground, the traffic halts and moves, and we try to make a living in-between somehow. We say we have no time to ask what matters. Soon that will be true.

We go inside to console ourselves, to make some poor soup of our ambitions, and watch the television. It will tell us what to buy. It will assure us we're okay watching like this, and that what's being sold is what we've been waiting for.

Who notices anymore the light of the dawn? Who listens to the silence? Who feels the wind or stands beneath the stars?

Out on the sea, the invincible sea, our debris collects in floating islands stretching out to the horizon and we don't really care. Are we worthy of this place?

We want our children to have a better life than ours, but their lives are already tainted by our restlessness and the mistakes that came before us. We hope for them but we don't know what we hope for.

Under a bridge in Paris a farmer from Morocco stretches a cloth to protect his family. Their baby is not comforted by the thunder of tires above.

Surely, we say, it is not as bad as all that. Surely our pleasantness will redeem us. Surely one day we will clean all this up and beauty will return to us and the little sparkles of light on the river will be enough to give us peace.

At this time of year the dark comes early. We pull the curtains and wait in our homes for something good to happen, even though it already has.

We mustn't fall asleep with these bleak thoughts. Let us say instead our most tender prayers, the first prayers of our heart. In the name of all that is most dear to us, let us re-dedicate our lives to the beauty we forget. In the name of all that has been hurt, let us vow to love what we love and give that to each other.

Bittersweet

ONE MORNING, GOD KNOWS WHY, you are swept clean of yourself. Wonder of wonders! Clear-headed and clear-hearted, you look around.

Things appear as they always have, and yet... you feel a kind of awe everywhere, a silent wondrous clarity spilling invisibly out of the moment.

You sense it's not an amazement private to you — it's everywhere! It's the awe at the start of things, the awe of the fact that anything shows up at all! What can you say about it, this pure radiant generosity? It gives the light in the trees outside your window, and in your eyes, and in the seeing of your eyes. Wonder is its nature — wonder is not just your response to it — your wonder is its wonder!

You feel your heart bursting with gladness. Now you know what the poet Yehuda Amichai meant when he wrote:

Behind all this some great happiness is hiding.

For you — for this moment — the great happiness has come out of hiding. You can't describe it because it's what you're made of. The great happiness is just how the moment pours forth, awesome and ordinary and not-even-here. You see the phenomena of the world appearing like the play and display of this great happiness — an infinite cornucopia spilling forth supernovas and galaxies and a universe filled with light all the way down to the delicate primrose in your garden.

But immediately you sense something else, something coming from within the great happiness — it's like a cry, a cry so poignant it has no sound. You know this soundless sound. You've known it for a long time. You can hardly bear it.

It's the silent cry of the world. Not just the cry of tragedy, though it's that too. It's old. It comes with the world. It comes with being the world. It's the cry of things mattering, of grief and pain. Bombs drop and splinter through children. An antelope succumbs to the lion's teeth and the herd runs on without her. An old abbey is torn down to make room for a tourist hotel. A white-haired man sits in the park missing his wife, dead these five years. It's the silent cry of things passing, things that matter.

Now you know what the Chan master John Hurrell Crook meant when he wrote:

Perhaps, ultimately, there is only a great sadness…

The great sadness pierces your heart while the great happiness frees it. Jesus wept, though he knew the truth. Contemplating the world, enlightened Buddha shed that single tear. You know there's no point in turning your heart to just one or the other — the great sadness and the great happiness come together. They are not to be resolved — they don't ask for that.

You know what they ask. They ask simply that you accept them, that you accept being pierced and freed by them in the same way you accept your sacred mortal body.

What candle shall we light, on what altar,
to this that lights the candle,
and is the candle, and the light?

Thanks

As THIS LITTLE BOOK GOES TO PRESS my last act is to write a few words of gratitude for the help I have received in its creation. But everything I have ever experienced and everything I have ever done has been given to me — this body, this breath, these thoughts, these feelings, the movement of this pen, even this sense of being a recipient of all this — a *me* — all of it has been given! So where shall I start with my gratitude? I cannot encompass it in words, my heart is overflowing with thanks. Mother, father, partners, lovers, children, teachers, friends, everyone who has ever taken care of me, loved me, inspired me, disagreed with me, worked and played with me, all of you my guides, all of you this endlessly generous radiance of the One Light, thank you!

And to name names, in particular I want to thank my friend Jeff Fuller who was often the first person to read early drafts of these pieces and who offered wise and incisive suggestions. My wife, Elizabeth Rabia Roberts, did the same, and my tender thanks to her for her love and for putting up with me all these years, and for her constant inspiration. Thanks to Mehera Bakker for her encouragement to gather these writings into a book, and thanks for the friendship and editorial help of Carol Barrow, Kiran and Jeanne Rana, Amrita Skye Blaine, Boudewijn Boom, and Ian Bill Scheffel, and to Connie Shaw at Sentient for making the publication of *Free Medicine* effortless. Finally, profound thanks to all those who cared to read these writings over the years — it was because of you that my pen moved at all.

Permissions

About the Author

ELIAS AMIDON IS THE SPIRITUAL DIRECTOR (Pir) of the Sufi
Way International, a non-sectarian mystical order in the lineage of
Sufi Inayat Khan. An initiate of the Sufi Way for the past forty-seven
years, Pir Elias has studied with Qadiri Sufis in Morocco, Theravadan
Buddhist teachers in Thailand, Native American teachers of the
Assemblies of the Morning Star, Christian monks in Syria, Zen
teachers of the White Plum Sangha, and contemporary teachers in
the Dzogchen tradition.

Elias has lived a multifaceted, engaged life, working as a school-
teacher, carpenter, architect, writer, environmental educator, peace

activist, and wilderness rites-of-passage guide. He helped develop several schools, including the Boulder Institute for Nature and the Human Spirit, the Institute for Deep Ecology, the graduate program in Environmental Leadership at Naropa University, and the Open Path. Co-editor of the books *Earth Prayers, Life Prayers,* and *Prayers for a Thousand Years,* he has worked for many years with his wife, Elizabeth Rabia Roberts, as a citizen activist for peace and interfaith understanding in Iraq, Syria, Afghanistan, Iran, Pakistan, and Israel/Palestine, and with indigenous tribes in Thailand and Burma on issues of cultural continuity and land rights (see: www.pathofthefriend.org). He was instrumental in founding the *Masar Ibrahim Al Khalil* (the Abraham Path), an international project dedicated to helping Middle Eastern countries open a network of cultural routes and walking trails throughout the region.

Pir Elias has been leading programs in Sufism for over three decades, and Open Path programs since 2005. He is the author of *The Open Path: Recognizing Nondual Awareness,* also published by Sentient Publications. Nine- and six-month Open Path Trainings are offered frequently in the United States, England, Holland, Germany, and Austria. These trainings give participants a chance to work directly with Elias over an extended period, learning to recognize and sustain the freshness of nondual awareness in their lives. One and two week solitary Open Path retreats are also held frequently at Nada Hermitage in Crestone, Colorado.

Information about current Open Path/Sufi Way programs can be found at www.sufiway.org.

Sentient Publications, LLC publishes nonfiction books on cultural creativity, experimental education, transformative spirituality, holistic health, new science, ecology, and other topics, approached from an integral viewpoint. We also publish fiction that aims to intrigue, stimulate, and entertain. Our authors are intensely interested in exploring the nature of life from fresh perspectives, addressing life's great questions, and fostering the full expression of the human potential. Sentient Publications' books arise from the spirit of inquiry and the richness of the inherent dialogue between writer and reader.

Our Culture Tools series is designed to give social catalyzers and cultural entrepreneurs the essential information, technology, and inspiration to forge a sustainable, creative, and compassionate world.

We are very interested in hearing from our readers. To direct suggestions or comments to us, or to be added to our mailing list, please contact:

SENTIENT PUBLICATIONS, LLC

PO Box 7204
Boulder, CO 80306
303-443-2188
contact@sentientpublications.com
www.sentientpublications.com